28 Hymns to Sing
Before You Die

28 Hymns to Sing
Before You Die

JOHN M. MULDER
and F. MORGAN ROBERTS

With a Foreword by Eugene H. Peterson

 CASCADE *Books* • Eugene, Oregon

28 HYMNS TO SING BEFORE YOU DIE

Cascade Books
An Imprint of Wipf and Stock Publishers
199 W. 8th Ave., Suite 3
Eugene, OR 97401

ISBN 13: 978-1-62564-149-6

Cataloguing-in-Publication data:

Mulder, John M. and F. Morgan Roberts

28 hymns to sing before you die / John M. Mulder and F. Morgan Roberts ; with a Foreword by Eugene H. Peterson.

xxii + 206 pp. ; 23 cm.

ISBN 13: 978-1-62564-149-6

1. Hymns, English—History and criticism. 2. Meditations. I. Title.

BV350 .H95 2014

Manufactured in the U.S.A.

John M. Mulder dedicates this book to his siblings,
Janel, Nancy, Mary, Andy, North, and Robin
who learned these hymns with him.

F. Morgan Roberts dedicates this book to his mother,
who would sing hymns as she ironed our clothes,
and to his father, who died with a hymn on his lips.

Contents

Acknowledgments   ix

Foreword by Eugene H. Peterson   xi

Introduction   xv

1   The Day of Resurrection   2

2   All Glory, Laud, and Honor   10

3   Jesus, the Very Thought of Thee   16

4   O Sacred Head, Now Wounded   24

5   A Mighty Fortress Is Our God   32

6   Now Thank We All Our God   40

7   When I Survey the Wondrous Cross   48

8   Jesus Shall Reign Where'er the Sun   58

9   Our God, Our Help in Ages Past   64

10   O for a Thousand Tongues to Sing   70

11   Christ the Lord Is Risen Today   80

12   Love Divine, All Loves Excelling   86

13   Come, Thou Almighty King   92

14   Guide Me, O Thou Great Jehovah   98

15   All Hail the Power of Jesus' Name   106

16   Glorious Things of Thee Are Spoken   114

17   Amazing Grace—How Sweet the Sound   122

18   How Firm a Foundation   130

19   Holy, Holy, Holy   138

20   In the Cross of Christ I Glory   146

21   O Worship the King   152

22   Savior, Like a Shepherd Lead Us   158

23   Just As I Am, Without One Plea   164

24   Come, Ye Thankful People, Come   170

25   Abide With Me   178

26   Crown Him With Many Crowns   186

27   There's a Wideness in God's Mercy   192

28   The Church's One Foundation   200

Acknowledgments

This book is the result of a friendship which began more than thirty years ago. We met on the campus of Louisville Presbyterian Theological Seminary, where John was a callow youth and totally inexperienced President, and where Morgan was a seasoned pastor and a wise and trusted member of the Board of Trustees. Our relationship quickly deepened, and over the years we have seen each other through great joys and "through many dangers, toils, and snares." Although our prose is presented separately, this is truly our book written together.

John thanks the libraries of Hope College, Louisville Seminary, and Western Theological Seminary and the website, www.hymnary.org that provided the historical background for each of the hymns. He is grateful to Second Presbyterian Church and St. Matthews Episcopal Church, both in Louisville, where he presented much of this material in an earlier form. His wife Mary earned her doctorate in English rhetoric and composition and taught English composition classes in two community colleges for more than thirty years. He has learned to rely on her corrections and insightful comments because she is an experienced expert; without her help, his writing would resemble the complexities of a Bach fugue.

Morgan thanks his wife, Nora, who patiently proof read his writing and encouraged him in his reflections and ruminations about some of Christianity's most eloquent expressions of faith.

We owe special thanks to Dirk Wierenga for supplying us with the whimsical and inspired title to our book.

Half of the honoraria for this book will go to Redlands Christian Migrant Association, 402 West Main Street, Immokalee, Florida 34142. Through its two charter schools in Immokalee and

Acknowledgments

Wimauma, and its eighty-seven child care centers, it serves more than 8,000 farm worker children annually.

For those who want accompaniment as they read or sing these hymns, music will be available on a CD at www.28hymns tosingbeforeyoudie.com or through music distribution sites.

Both of us have loved hymns all of our lives, and so preparing this book was fun. As you read it, we hope you will see the passion and commitment of the poets and composers. Most of all, we hope it will inspire you to sing God's praises and walk the path God has illumined for you.

John M. Mulder

F. Morgan Roberts

Foreword

Eugene H. Peterson

Isaac Watts (died 1748), the "father of English hymnody," from an early age loved to make words rhyme. When he was caught with his eyes open during family prayers, he replied:

> A little mouse for want of stairs
> Ran up a rope to say his prayers.

This annoyed his father who spanked him and warned him to stop rhyming. Isaac reportedly replied,

> Oh, father, do some pity take
> And I will no more verses make.

But he didn't keep his word. It wasn't long before he had given up child rhymes for rhymes that sang the praise and presence of God. During his lifetime he wrote about 750 hymns. Previous to Watts, people sang the Psalms almost exclusively. Along with most of my contemporaries, I grew up singing the twenty-eight hymns included in this book, although not to the exclusion of the Psalms. I have sung these hymns in many congregations, many times throughout my life.

I still have a clear remembrance of learning how a hymnbook worked. I would stand on a church pew beside my father—I was just learning to read—as he patiently instructed me in how to read the words under the musical notes line by line, separately, and not as I was being taught to read books in school. In the church culture in which I grew up, most Christian homes had a well-used hymnbook as well as a Bible in view. My mother always had a hymnbook on her ironing board as she did her best to keep my siblings and me appearing respectable as we went to school and church. Yet in fifty years of making pastoral calls, I can only recall twice seeing a hymnbook out in the open where it looks like it might have been used lately. Hymns were part of the culture.

But within my lifetime that has changed. Many congregations no longer use hymnbooks, using instead projections on an illuminated screen. I have a good friend, now retired. All his life he has been a pastor in his denomination that is well known for its rapid growth around the world. He has a good voice, loves to sing, and mostly loves to sing in a congregation where the hymns that are in this book are sung. But Sundays have become a trial for him. The music is loud, irreverent, and repetitive. In his denomination the word on the street is that hymns are no longer in vogue. They have been replaced by what some have named the Seven-Eleven Songbook: seven words, repeated eleven times.

John Mulder and Morgan Roberts, pooling their historical insights and pastoral imagination, are giving us a second chance at recovering treasures that will reinvigorate our worship. It helps to know the historical and cultural conditions in which these hymns came into being. And it helps to have a pastor reflect freshly on half-forgotten (maybe) revelation.

Before reading this book, I knew very little of the men and women responsible for these hymns, the conditions in which they were written and translated. The conditions were not exactly propitious.

Each of these hymns is an act of worship that brings us into an awareness and receptivity to the life of the Trinity—the operations of all the persons of the Trinity in a participatory way. But the conditions in which they were composed and sung were more often than not pain and devastation, sickness and poverty. And yet, somehow beauty and elegance were distilled out of conditions of doubt and hopelessness.

To begin with, Martin Rinkart (died 1649). This German pastor wrote "Now Thank We All Our God" in the midst of the Thirty Years' War. He lived all his life in Eilenburg, a walled city in Germany. Because of the mass killing outside the walls and the famine, disease, and plague within the walls, the outbreak of disease was so bad that sometimes Rinkart preached burial sermons for forty to fifty people in one day. Eventually, all the pastors in the city died except Rinkart. That was the world in which he wrote "Now Thank We All Our God."

Lacking the medical technology that we take for granted, many of these hymn writers were ill and infirm much of their lives. Isaac Watts, who leads the parade, was unable to work throughout his adult life and was cared for by the Lord Mayor of London and his wife.

Charlotte Elliot's famous hymn, "Just as I Am," was written from the depths of chronic illness and depression. She lived a long life (82 years) but at the age of thirty-two was stricken with illness that left her a semi-invalid for the rest of her life.

And Charles Wesley, plagued with illness his entire life, still managed to write 6,500 hymns.

One of the huge ironies that never fails to surprise me is that these very hymns that have brought consolation and joy and peace to so many also ignited a bitter fight between the Psalm Singers (who held that the only thing people should sing is the words of the Bible, meaning mostly the Psalms) and the Hymn Singers (who argued that if you only sang the Psalms you had to leave out Christ and the entire New Testament). Eventually the Hymn Singers prevailed, but it took fifty years.

In this book we are given an anecdote about how bitter this fight was here in America. In 1789 the Reverend Adam Rankin rode on horseback from his congregation in Kentucky to the first General Assembly of the Presbyterian Church in the United States of America. He pleaded with his fellow Presbyterians to refuse to allow "the great and pernicious error of adopting the use of Watts' hymns in public worship in preference to versifications of the Psalms of David." The Assembly listened and "in a model of Christian charity, encouraged him to be kind to those who disagreed and to cease disturbing the peace of the church on the issue of hymns."

The argument and fight lasted for nearly a half-century. Mulder comments: "It's striking that about every fifty to one hundred years there is a fight about music in the church. We saw it again in the nineteenth century when gospel hymns were introduced and then in the twentieth and early twenty-first centuries with the rise of 'contemporary Christian worship.'"

We have a rich tradition of singing in our Scriptures, embraced at the beginning by the singing of Moses and Miriam at the Red Sea (Exod 15) and at the ending by the singing of four living creatures, the twenty-four elders, and the seven angels in Revelation (chapters 4–5, 15).

G. K. Chesterton once defined tradition as giving a vote to our ancestors. Think of John Mulder and Morgan Roberts as casting votes for the *28 Hymns* on our behalf.

Eugene H. Peterson
Professor Emeritus of Spiritual Theology
Regent College
Vancouver, B.C.

Introduction

"I remember more hymns than I do sermons."

Preachers hear that verdict with chagrin, but in unguarded moments, they often make the same judgment. Hymns are memorable—partly for the poetry, partly for the music. They stick in people's memories. In fact, hymns probably shape the faith and piety of more people than any other Christian expression.

Hymns weren't always part of the life of English-speaking churches. But beginning in the eighteenth century and continuing into the twenty-first century, hymns have become the dominant feature of the music in English-speaking Protestant churches and other churches as well.

At the same time, most churchgoers sing hymns without a clue about where the words and music came from or what they might mean. This little book is designed to address that ignorance by outlining the history of a hymn and by offering meditations about how a hymn might both inform and inspire followers of Jesus today.

We focus on the twenty-seven hymns that have appeared most often in the main Protestant hymnals since the late nineteenth century—plus "Amazing Grace," which makes twenty-eight. You might be surprised that "Amazing Grace" didn't make the "hit parade of hymns." Actually, until relatively recently, "Amazing Grace" was not particularly popular in Britain, despite its stupendous popularity in the U.S.

We came to our list of twenty-eight hymns "to sing before you die" by relying on the research of Robert T. Coote, published in *Christianity Today* in March 2011. Coote provided our canon of canticles, and we are deeply grateful to him for his prodigious achievement. Spending two years, he surveyed 4,905 hymns from the hymnbooks of six mainline Protestant denominations:

- Anglican (Episcopal), four editions, from 1892
- American Baptist, four editions, from 1883
- Congregational (United Church of Christ), five editions, from 1897
- Evangelical Lutheran Church in America, five editions, from 1899
- United Methodist, five editions, from 1878
- Presbyterian Church (USA), five editions, from 1885

Hymns had to appear in at least twenty-six of the twenty-eight hymnals in Coote's survey, and they had to be included in the hymnbooks currently in use by those denominations.

As another indication of the popularity of these hymns, Coote also looked at six widely-used evangelical hymnbooks (*Christian Life Hymnal, Celebration Hymnal, Trinity Hymnal, Hymnal for Worship and Celebration, Hymns for the Family of God,* and *Hymns for the Living Church*). Each of the twenty-eight hymns appeared in every hymnbook except two.

Roman Catholics avidly sing hymns today, largely as a result of the worship reforms of Vatican II in the 1960s. What seemed for centuries as an unbridgeable division between Catholics and Protestants is now bridged by song. Of the twenty-eight hymns in this book, fifteen are included in *Gather Comprehensive* (2004), one of the most widely used Catholic hymnals.

In a study of sixty-seven Catholic hymnbooks, twelve of our twenty-eight hymns are among the twenty-three most popular among Catholics.

As a Catholic friend told us, "When we were told we could sing hymns, we didn't have very many. So we borrowed from you!"

We checked Coote's work against a much larger and exhaustive study of Stephen A. Marini, which ranked the most often reprinted hymns found in 175 American Protestant hymnals and hymn books published from 1737 to 1960. Because it used different criteria, it produced somewhat different but definitely complementary results. What is most surprising is how many hymns—once considered popular—have dropped from contemporary usage; for example, few today sing Isaac Watts' "Am I a Soldier of the Cross" or his "When I Can Read My Title Clear" or "There Is a Land of Pure Delight."

Using Coote's criteria, it's inevitable that many favorites did not make the cut for this book. Christmas carols, choruses, and service music were not included in the final list because they are different than hymns. Black spirituals weren't sung in white churches until the mid-twentieth century. Gospel songs were only beginning to make their impact on Protestant church life by the end of the nineteenth century. And the twentieth century has seen an explosion of hymn writing, not to speak of the songs of "contemporary Christian worship."

Other criteria would produce a different list, and yet, these twenty-eight hymns appear again and again in worship, testifying by their endurance to their power to speak about the Christian faith—eloquently, persuasively, memorably.

In this book, we include both the words and the music for each hymn, using the tune that is most often associated with that hymn. Then John M. Mulder provides some historical background to the hymn's composition, followed by a meditation by F. Morgan Roberts on what the hymn might mean to today's Christians.

Both of us are ordained ministers in the Presbyterian Church (USA). Both of us have preached a lot of sermons, but for us hymns resound in our hearts and minds. In writing this book, we've discovered that the historical setting for a hymn makes it even more moving and inspiring, and the meditations are an invitation to reflect on how these hymns resound across the years to help us walk in God's path with the illumination of divine light and sacred song.

As we worked together and discussed these twenty-eight hymns, we noticed some themes that ran through the words penned by poets.

- *The sovereignty of God.* This is often expressed as kingship, lordship, sovereignty, God's greatness, the final victory of God's kingdom, etc. Examples abound: "All Glory, Laud, and Honor," "All Hail the Power of Jesus' Name," "Christ, the Lord, Is Risen Today," "Come, Ye Thankful People, Come," "Come, Thou Almighty King," "Guide Me, O Thou Great Jehovah," "Crown Him With Many Crowns," "In the Cross of Christ I Glory," "Jesus Shall Reign," and many more.

  As we note in this book, kingship seems like a strange theme in religious song in America—a nation that threw off monarchy and embraced democracy. And yet, it may be that the idea of a sovereign Lord was and remains relevant for a people who too often embrace the idea that their prosperity and fortunes are the result of their own labors. Too often we are fixated on creating and preserving our own security, for ourselves, for our families, for our nation, and these themes of God's power are a healthy dose of humility and a reminder of our dependence upon God for our very existence and the meaning of life.

  One of us talked with a Christian who had suffered terrible losses in the stock market crash of 2008. When asked how he felt, he replied simply, "It wasn't mine to begin with."

  We need a strong dose of God's sovereignty, and these hymns could be the medicine we need.

- *God's presence amidst uncertainty and suffering.* All of these hymns come from an age in which life was far less certain that it is today. We have medical technology that makes our lives longer and recovery from disease more certain. We have weaponry beyond the imagination of our great grandparents to secure our nation. We have information technology that relieves our uncertainty about so many of life's questions.

  And yet, with so many people living in anxiety, these writers composed out of and about how God's presence invades our weakness and offers strength. A striking number of these hymns were written by ailing people from the depths of illness. Consider only two examples.

Isaac Watts spent nearly his entire adult life as an invalid, but from his heart and mind exploded hundreds of hymns, including this heroic, humble affirmation:

> Were the whole realm of nature mine,
> That were a present far too small;
> Love so amazing, so divine,
> Demands my soul, my life my all.

Charlotte Elliott's famous hymn, "Just As I Am," was written from depths of chronic illness and depression. In fact, it might be said that she never would have written the hymn without her suffering and illness. But, aware of God's presence, she proclaimed:

> Just as I am, though tossed about
> With many a conflict, many a doubt,
> Fightings and fears within, without,
> O Lamb of God, I come, I come.

There is a disturbing but compelling truth that we do not come to God without a recognition of our own weakness and fallibility. We are not God. We cannot save ourselves. And so often this realization comes through illness.

Contemporary sermons often proclaim *God's deliverance*—beyond death or within one's psyche. These hymns may also sound those notes, but they are also ringing affirmations that *God's presence* is not merely within us or beyond this life but in our lives and the life of the world as we confront it each day. God's love is now.

- *The breadth of God's grace and mercy.* Every epoch of the church's history has seen attempts to define who is a Christian and what is right belief or behavior. That is inevitable and even necessary. But it is also true that every heresy, every deviation from accepted orthodoxy and truth, is also a signal of something in the gospel of Christ that the church is forgetting or ignoring, something that breaks through the boundaries of our conviction and conventions.

For example, "The Church's One Foundation" was written in the midst theological polemics and acrimony. Even so, Samuel Sebastian Wesley wrote,

> Lord, give us grace that we,
> Like them, the meek and lowly,
> May live eternally.

Each of these hymns—in its own way—declares "There Is a Wideness in God's Mercy." God's family is much bigger than the church; God's children are drawn from across the globe; and despite all we have done or who we are, we belong to God. Surely the emphasis on God's mercy is at least part of the astounding and continuing popularity of "Amazing Grace":

> Through many dangers, toils, and snares,
> I have already come;
> 'Tis grace has brought me safe thus far,
> And grace shall lead me home.

This book can be used as an aid to corporate worship by church musicians, pastors, and congregations. Virtually every hymn in this book was written *from* a congregation *for* a congregation. As a result, hymns are inevitably experienced as a common talk about God and conversation with God. We learn hymns from one another, and some of the deepest experiences of God's love come in our singing together.

But we also hope this book will be especially used as an educational and devotional aid for individuals. The selections are short; they can be read before sleep descends or as morning dawns.

For us, hymns have sustained us through some of the most difficult periods of our lives. During one of those times, John Mulder sought solace in Scripture, which helped. He prayed deeply and fervently; that helped as well. But what consoled him, comforted him, and ultimately inspired him was silently singing favorite hymns that broke through the darkness and brought light, especially "The Lord's My Shepherd, I'll Not Want" to the tune of Crimond.

Morgan Roberts remembers that the last thing his father did was to sing a hymn. His father's memory was good, and he retained a keen mental grasp on the details of living until the very end. Then, on his last day, as his strength was fading, he said to Morgan's mother, "Bea, let's sing." When she asked him what he wanted to sing, he replied, "Let's sing 'Blessed Assurance.'" So they began to sing, and before they finished the hymn, he fell asleep—to awaken "on another shore, and in a brighter light."

There are many ways life can end, but one of the best scripts is: "Exit singing."

Together, we offer these hymns as a response to that ancient injunction: "Let the word of Christ dwell in you richly; teach and admonish one another in all wisdom; and with gratitude in your hearts sing psalms, hymns, and spiritual songs to God" (Col 3:16).

John M. Mulder and F. Morgan Roberts

28 Hymns to Sing
Before You Die

The Day of Resurrection

1 The day of res - ur - rec - tion! Earth, tell it out a - broad;
2 Our hearts be pure from e - vil, that we may see a - right
3 Now let the heavens be joy - ful, let earth its song be - gin,

the Pass - o - ver of glad - ness, the Pass - o - ver of God.
the Christ who reigns e - ter - nal in res - ur - rec - tion light;
the whole world keep high tri - umph, and all that is there - in;

From death to life e - ter - nal, from earth un - to the sky,
We lis - ten for the teach - ings once heard so calm and plain,
Let all things seen and un - seen their notes of glad - ness blend,

our Christ has brought us o - ver with hymns of vic - to - ry.
for we, too, want to fol - low and raise the vic - tor strain.
for Christ a - gain has ris - en, our joy that has no end.

1

The Day of Resurrection

This hymn was written by John of Damascus, who was born about 657 and died about 754. He was an eighth-century Greek theologian, hymn writer, and a Father of the Greek Church at Damascus.

One writer calls him "the most important dogmatist" (or defender of Christian doctrine) of the Eastern Orthodox Church. He was an eloquent writer and speaker, which earned him the title of "Stream of Gold." John Mason Neale, who translated this hymn, said John was "the last but one of the Fathers of the Greek Church, and the greatest of her poets" and called "The Day of Resurrection" the "glorious old hymn of victory."

John's father, who was a Christian, held an important official position at the court of the Muslim Caliph in Damascus. When his father died, John filled the position and became wealthy. When he was about forty, he became dissatisfied with his life and gave away his possessions, freed his slaves, and entered a monastery in the desert near Jerusalem. He then became a leading theologian of the Eastern Church and eventually was canonized by both the Eastern and Western Churches.

John also was a great defender of the church's use of icons. He codified the practices of Byzantine chant and wrote about science, philosophy, and theology.

He is known for writing six canons for the major festivals of the church year. A canon is a form of Greek hymnody based on biblical canticles, consisting of nine odes, each with six to nine stanzas.

All the canons of the Greek Church illustrate how the Old Testament prophecies were fulfilled in Christ's resurrection.

You can see that here in the first verse of the hymn with its reference to the Passover, and this hymn has become known as "the golden canon" or "the queen of canons."

John also wrote another familiar Easter hymn, "Come, Ye Faithful, Raise the Strain."

"The Day of Resurrection" was rather freely translated by John Mason Neale, one of the greatest contributors to our hymnody. In fact, in the Episcopal *Hymnal 1982*, there are forty-five hymns that in one way or another bear Neale's name—either as the author or as translator.

Neale was a member of a reform movement in the Church of England known as the Oxford Movement. It sought to return the church to some of its early and medieval roots, and because it drew its inspiration from the Orthodox and Roman Catholic traditions (in other words its Greek and Latin literature), it was very controversial. Yet Neale and a few others are almost solely responsible for bringing the richness of early and medieval Christianity into the modern church.

Neale's parents were ardent evangelicals, and their son was educated at Trinity College, Cambridge, and Downing College, where he excelled in all the disciplines—except mathematics. He eventually mastered twenty languages.

Because of the opposition of his superiors in the church and his severe lung problems, he spent almost his entire ministry as the warden of Sackville College, East Grinstead, London, which was actually a rescue mission for impoverished old men. Neale was the chaplain and survived on a miniscule salary of twenty-seven pounds annually. He was also one of the founders of an Anglican order, the Sisterhood of St. Margaret's, which did pioneering work among women and children.

We will see that Neale is one of several individuals who, despite physical pain and infirmity, had extraordinary ministries and produced verse and music that soared in beauty.

To get a sense of how this hymn was used in the lifetime of John of Damascus, here is one description:

"At 12:00 midnight on Easter Eve a cannon shot announces that Easter Day has begun. At that moment the Archbishop, elevating the cross, cries out 'Christ is risen!' Instantly the vast multitude, waiting in long silence, bursts forth in a shout of indescribable joy, 'Christ is risen! Christ is risen!' Then the oppressive darkness is succeeded by a blaze of light from a thousand tapers. Bands of music strike up their gayest strains. Everywhere men clasp each other's hands and embrace with countenances beaming with delight. And above the mingling of many sounds the priests can be heard chanting, 'The day of resurrection/Earth tell it out abroad.'"

The tune for this hymn is Lancashire, written by Henry Thomas Smart. It was originally intended for a hymn, "From Greenland's Icy Mountains," to be sung at a missionary meeting in Lancashire, England. (About this hymn, see p. 140.) Thus, its name.

Smart was born in 1813 and died in 1879. His first music teacher was his father, and then he continued on his own. He tried the practice of law for a while but turned to music for the rest of his life. He was an accomplished organist and achieved great reknown during his lifetime. He was also a gifted composer and hymn writer. He went completely blind at age fifty-two and thereafter dictated his hymns and music to his daughter.

As you sing this hymn, try to remember the sheer joy of those early Christians who, like John, discovered that the one who had died was now alive. Try to catch the missionary spirit that inspired the music and ponder anew what difference it makes in our lives that Jesus has been raised for us and for our world today.

Meditation

Eternal Springtime

The final words of this ancient hymn say it all, "Our joy that hath no end."

Unfortunately, however, Easter, the day of resurrection, has a somewhat abrupt ending in the worship practice of our churches. We sing our traditional Easter hymns, hopefully this great one, on Easter Sunday and, maybe also, on the Sunday after Easter, but after that, this hymn and other Easter hymns are tucked away for the rest of the year in the Easter section of our hymnbooks.

How sad that we think of Easter as a seasonal festival! We think of it as a very special feast of the church that comes in the spring of the year, with all the associations that go with the rites of spring. After all, how can we resist making such connections as winter ends and our trees and flowering plants seem to join in our celebration of resurrection and new life?

My guess is that we never sing this hymn during the rest of the year because, well, . . . it just doesn't fit in with summer, fall, and winter. Imagine singing it on a freezing winter morning in January; it just doesn't seem to work. But that's exactly when we ought to try singing it, on the darkest, coldest, and most hopeless mornings of our life, because the resurrection of Jesus can bring glory to all such gloomy mornings.

In another grand Easter hymn, John of Damascus, the author of this hymn, writes, "'Tis the spring of souls today; Christ hath burst his prison." That's the real association with spring that we're meant to celebrate at Easter; Jesus' resurrection has made us unendingly, in all seasons, a springtime people.

Because the risen Jesus is now living his resurrection life within our life, every morning is a fresh start, a new beginning. In the words of an old gospel hymn from my youth, I can sing, "There is springtime in my soul today."

I remember meeting an affluent couple who set out on a photographic pilgrimage. Their plan was to follow spring around the world, recording its beauty as it moved from east to west, north to south in different countries and continents. Even though I never got to view any of their photos, what glorious scenes they must have captured, and what memories they must surely continue to enjoy.

We have something better, even if we have never traveled more than one hundred miles from the place of our birth (which, actually, was the case with Jesus of Nazareth). Looking out of any window, even in the worst places on earth and on the worst mornings of human experience, we know that life is always beginning for us. Because of the resurrection, every day has some new possibility for me that has never existed before. If I will simply allow God to open my eyes, every day can become a spiritual safari into new adventures.

But as the tacky TV commercials say, "But wait, there's more!"

New life with Jesus is not only blessed with continual beginnings; it is never ending. The kind of eternal life that began at the empty tomb many centuries ago and continues to live in our life has no endings. We often feel sad when we come to the end of a really good book. And if it is the last book the author has written, then we feel really sad because we realize that there will be no more wonderful stories from this writer.

But human life is not like a good book that, finally, must come to an end.

No human life ever comes to an end! Sometimes it seems that way. The lives of all kinds of ordinary people appear to come to an end and be forgotten. Sometimes there are no family members left to visit their grave, cherish their memory, or keep some shred of remembrance alive. And, of course, there are also the bad people whose story, thankfully, has ended.

But the God who is the creator of every human life, good or bad, is also the God who brought again from the dead our

Lord, Jesus Christ. Somehow, somewhere, God will pursue every human life until God's unique and perfect plan is realized in every life. Heaven will not be heaven without you! Indeed, heaven will not be fully heaven until the story of every human life is brought to a joyful ending. And what a spring morning that will be when God is all, and in all!

Marv Hiles tells the entire story of Holy Week and Easter in one sentence: "A young rabbi walks to Jerusalem and disappears forever into springtime." It is with this rabbi Jesus that we are traveling!

All Glory, Laud, and Honor

1 All glo - ry, laud, and hon - or to you, Re - deem - er, King,
2 The com - pa - ny of an - gels is prais - ing you on high;
3 To you be - fore your pas - sion they sang their hymns of praise;

to whom the lips of chil - dren made sweet ho - san - nas ring.
and we with all cre - a - tion in cho - rus make re - ply.
to you, now high ex - alt - ed, our mel - o - dy we raise.

You are the King of Is - ra - el and Da - vid's roy - al Son,
The peo - ple of the He - brews with palms be - fore you went;
As you re - ceived their prais - es, ac - cept the prayers we bring,

now in the Lord's name com - ing, the King and Bless - ed One.
our praise and prayer and an - thems be - fore you we pre - sent.
for you de - light in good - ness, O good and gra - cious King!

2

All Glory, Laud, and Honor

This hymn comes about a century after "The Day of Resurrection." The approximate date is around 820. It was
written by Theodulph, the bishop of Orleans. Theodulph was
a child of Italian nobility but chose a life of religious service
instead. At first he was an abbot of a monastery in Florence, and
in 781 Charlemagne appointed him Bishop of Orleans.

His career came to an abrupt stop when Charlemagne died.
King Louis I or King Louis the Pious thought Theodulph was
part of a plot to overthrow him and sent him to jail in Angiers
in 818. While he was imprisoned in France he apparently wrote
this hymn, and he died three years later, probably from poison.

The following is perhaps an apocryphal tale from the sixteenth century, but it's a good one nonetheless.

The story goes that King Louis was passing the prison
where Theodulph was incarcerated. As he passed, he heard
Theodulph singing this hymn. Apparently the king was so
moved that he liberated Theodolph. Not only that, he issued a
decree that "All Glory, Laud, and Honor" should be sung on all
subsequent Palm Sundays.

The text was translated by John Mason Neale, whose
renditions have given us so many gorgeous hymns from the
ancient and medieval churches. Because of Neale's magnificent
work in the nineteenth century, here are only some of the more
than 100 beautiful hymns he rescued from historical obscurity
and brought to us: "O Come, O Come, Emmanuel" (from the
twelfth century), "Good Christian Friends, Rejoice" (from the
medieval Latin), "Come, Ye Thankful, Raise the Strain" (from
the eighth century), "Of the Father's Love Begotten" (from the

fifth century), and "Christ Is Made the Sure Foundation" (from the seventh century). From his own hand, he gave us "Good King Wenceslas."

Incidentally, despite his minimal salary and impoverished life, Neale never accepted any royalties from his musical labors. He died before he reached the age of fifty.

Although Neale was ordained as a parish priest, he was unable to carry out ministerial tasks and spent his life in semi-invalidism. This gave him time for his prodigious historical and theological work. He railed against the theology of Isaac Watts' hymns, about which we will read more later (see pp. 49–50). He also attacked the seizure of church land throughout Christian history, arguing that the revenues of such land were diverted from alleviating the plight of the poor. In short, Neale was something more than an antiquarian but a man with compassion for those who were suffering like him.

Neale's work is testimony to the famous adage: "From the fires of the past, bring the coals, not the ashes."

This hymn is based on Matthew 21:1–11 as well as similar passages in Mark, Luke, and John, and it is clearly intended as a Palm Sunday celebration—both in ancient days and our own. Today it is used in both Protestant and Roman Catholic churches.

The tune is called "Valet Will Ich Dir Geben" or sometimes "St. Theodulph" (although there is no evidence that Theodulph was ever elevated to sainthood). It was composed by Melchior Teschner, a seventeenth-century Polish/German pastor and composer who wrote this originally as a musical setting for the dying. Johannes Sebastian Bach used this chorale in his "St. John's Passion."

The harmonization was provided by William H. Monk during the nineteenth century. Monk was a towering figure in church music of the nineteenth century as a choir director. He was the first music editor of *Hymns Ancient and Modern*, the Anglican hymnal that sold sixty million copies.

And so, you have it: a Palm Sunday hymn to celebrate Jesus Christ as King, written by a man imprisoned for his faith, just like the Apostle Paul. It was translated by an impoverished minister who spent his life caring for destitute men and women. It is sung to music intended as comfort for dying people. In short, this is a hymn that reminds us of Christ's majesty and our frailty, and it's a hymn of comfort for those who suffer.

Meditation

Choose Your Parade

If you had your "druthers" where would you want to worship on Palm Sunday? Most of you will probably say that, best of all, you'd want to be in your "home church," the one where you worship regularly. If, however, you're not completely satisfied with that church, your answer might be that, on that special holy day, you wish you could somehow return to the beloved church of your childhood.

But let's say that you're away from home on a business trip, that Palm Sunday finds you alone in a hotel in strange city, and that you must choose some church right where you are this morning. What kind of church will you choose for this special day that begins Holy Week?

Over the years I've worshiped in all kinds of churches on Palm Sunday, the "tall steeple" churches where this day is celebrated with grand music and high pageantry, but also the little ones where simplicity is the style on every Sunday. After all these years, my choice would be determined by the rule, "the smaller and simpler the better."

I hope that those of you who enjoy the inspiring grandeur of a magnificent sanctuary, classical church music, and high liturgical regalia won't feel that I'm putting you and your church down. What I hope all of us will realize, whatever the size and style of our regular place of worship, is that we reflect upon the fact that too much pomp and circumstance can be somehow "out of sync" with what happened on that first Palm Sunday.

An accurate translation of that first Palm Sunday into contemporary imagery would have us see Jesus, making his entrance into Jerusalem, standing on the bed of a small, dirty pickup truck, just a plain work vehicle which, after all, is what a donkey was in that ancient world.

Of course, reading the Gospel account with that imagery in mind might spoil the glitzy show that we're tempted to make of this day. And maybe that's why our hymnals have never included one of the verses that Theodulph wrote for this hymn. We never sing the quatrain that would have us declare:

> Be thou, O Lord, the rider
> And we the little ass,
> That to God's holy city
> Together we may pass.

Making this day too grandiose just won't work with those words. Maybe Theodulph was trying to tell us something that we've been missing all along, telling us about the kind of king Jesus wanted to be.

How could we have missed what the prophet Zechariah warned us was coming? "Lo, your king comes to you; triumphant and victorious is he, humble and riding on a donkey, on a colt, the foal of a donkey" (Zech 9:9).

That's not the kind of a king or kingdom we were expecting. To see real royalty, we need only look at the parade entering Jerusalem at the other end of the city that day. As Jesus arrived from the east, the Roman governor, Pontius Pilate, was entering the city from the west.

No little asses in that assemblage! Here was imperial power, coming to insure that there would be peace during the upcoming celebration of Passover, the Roman kind of peace, Pax

Romana, the stability achieved by naked, overwhelming power. The armor and weapons of war, plus the sounds of marching feet and horses' hooves tell us that this was a real kingdom, standing tall in military might. But it's not the kind of kingdom, the kind of empire, that Jesus proclaimed.

The kind of parade that Jesus brought to town that day represented the arrival of a new kind of government for the world, the kind of reign in which worldly empires would be upturned so that our world could begin to look like God were king. The parade of Jesus was ushering in the reign of God's love and justice. No wonder the peasants were cheering! At last, it was their day.

But there's the problem. The peasants waiting along the road for Jesus' entry weren't "dressed to the nines" as many of us will be on Palm Sunday. They were not "our kind" of people, and we're not the kind of people who want to be thought of as little asses.

It's hard enough singing the metrical version of Psalm 23 in which we are taught to think of ourselves as "poor little lambs who've lost our way." We really don't want to look like sheep— and we certainly don't want to be thought of as little asses.

But this is the choice thrust upon us by the true meaning of Palm Sunday. We've got to choose the parade we'll join. It doesn't have anything to do with the kind of church we choose. Any ordinary disciple in any ordinary church can join Jesus' parade.

But it does mean becoming a different kind of disciple and working to make our church a different kind of church. It means making our entire way of life match the parade that Jesus is leading.

I'm not comfortable with the notion of becoming one of the little asses that travels with Jesus. However, it's better than ending up like Pontius Pilate. The verdict of history, after all, is that Jesus was a greater King than Pontius Pilate ever hoped to be. I'm choosing, difficult as it will be, to march with Jesus.

Jesus, the Very Thought of Thee

1. Je - sus, the ve - ry thought of thee
2. O hope of ev - ery con - trite heart,
3. But what to those who find? Ah, this
4. Je - sus, our on - ly joy be thou,

with sweet - ness fills the breast; but swee - ter far thy
O joy of all the meek, to those who fall, how
nor tongue nor pen can show; the love of Je - sus,
as thou our prize wilt be; Je - sus, be thou our

face to see, and in thy pre - sence rest.
kind thou art! How good to those who seek!
what it is, none but his loved ones know.
glo - ry now, and through e - ter - ni - ty.

3

Jesus, the Very Thought of Thee

This moving hymn was reputedly written by Bernard of Clairvaux, who was born to nobility in 1090 and died in 1153. Even though scholars have demonstrated that the hymn was probably written by an Englishman at the beginning of the twelfth century, it is still traditionally attributed to Bernard because it captures so much of his faith and piety.

Born to wealth and privilege, Bernard nevertheless took on a life of poverty. He entered the new order of the Cistercians after the death of his mother when he was only nineteen. While not its founder, Bernard became the primary builder of the Cistercian order, known in part for its famous offshoot, the Trappists.

The monastery at Gesthemane in Kentucky is part of the Trappist order, and Thomas Merton, perhaps the most influential spiritual writer of the twentieth century, is Gesthemane's most famous monk.

Bernard established the Cistercian monastery of Clairvaux, and thus he is known to history as Bernard of Clairvaux. He was handsome and renowned for his eloquence in preaching and persuasion. During his lifetime, he exercised huge influence in both the church and politics and became an adviser to popes and kings.

He served as one of the chief apologists for the Crusades, and when the Second Crusade failed, he was bitterly disappointed. In addition, he helped design the Rule of the Knights Templar.

He spent forty years in the cloister and died at age sixty-three. He was the first Cistercian monk to be named a saint and was also given the title "Doctor of the Church."

At the heart of his ministry were self-giving, Christian character, and evangelical zeal. He sought to take the sacramental and liturgical life of the church and transfer it into the lives of Christians. "Knowing God," he wrote, "is a matter of the heart."

From his youth he had a great love of literature, especially poetry, and he sought to make the Bible accessible to the average person through poetry. He had an abiding devotion to the Virgin Mary, which was central to the revival of Christian piety during the twelfth century.

He is sometimes considered a Protestant before the Protestants, despite his veneration of the Virgin Mary. Bernard, according to Martin Luther, was "the best monk that ever lived, whom I admire beyond all the rest put together."

Despite his Mariology, Bernard fought against the doctrine of the Immaculate Conception of Mary. He advocated forcefully for the doctrine of justification by faith. That, of course, was the rallying cry of the Reformers, especially Luther and Calvin. Luther called the doctrine of justification the foundation of the church, without which the church stands or falls.

That should remind us that the Reformers did not seek a new faith or a new church but a renewal of the church based on the Bible and the teachings of the church—in this case, a reforming monk who lived 400 years before the Reformation.

Bernard's hymn was translated by Edward Caswell (1814–1878), a nineteenth-century priest in the Church of England. Like John Mason Neale, he was part of the Oxford movement that sought to revitalize the church through its ancient and medieval traditions.

Unlike Neale, he eventually converted to Roman Catholicism and wrote many hymns for Catholic use. After his wife's death, he was ordained as a Catholic priest. He aligned himself with Cardinal John Henry Newman in Birmingham, where he combined hymn-writing with a ministry to impoverished children.

The tune, "St. Agnes," is frequently used with this hymn. It was originally called "St. Agnes, Durham." St. Agnes was a thirteen-year-old Roman martyr of the fourth century. According to tradition, the young Agnes was sentenced to death for refusing to marry a nobleman. She declared, "I am already engaged *to Christ*; to Him alone I keep my troth."

The composer is John Bacchus Dykes (1823–1876), an English musician who wrote this tune in 1862. Dykes was a musical prodigy. At the age of ten, he was assistant organist in his grandfather's church. He studied at Cambridge University for the priesthood, and while he was there he cofounded the Cambridge University Musical Society.

After his ordination, he served various churches, mostly in Durham, and this is why the tune was originally named "St. Agnes, Durham." Dykes died when he was only fifty-three, but during his short life he composed more than 300 hymn tunes, and sixty were used in the first edition of the hugely influential *Hymns Ancient and Modern* (1861).

This hymn was written to make Jesus come alive in our hearts and our entire being. This is not a Jesus of thought or doctrine but Jesus as the source of our life and action. Bernard wanted to take the Jesus of history and make him personal—the savior of our hearts and minds today.

The historian Philip Schaff declared that "Jesus, the Very Thought of Thee" was "the sweetest and most evangelical . . . hymn of the Middle Ages." David Livingstone, the great English missionary and explorer of Africa, wrote in his diary that "the hymn of St. Bernard, on the name of Christ, . . . pleases me so; it rings in my ears as I wander across the wide, wide wilderness." May it also be so on all our journeys.

Meditation

God Alone

Even if this hymn was not written by Bernard of Clairvaux, its monastic spirit makes it feel as though it must have been the work of someone who had chosen such a way of life. Who but someone who had left the secular world to devote one's entire life to the search for God in the silent world of Benedictine discipline could have prayed, "Jesus, our only joy be Thou"?

However devout we may be as ordinary Christians, we do have other legitimate joys; Jesus is not quite our "only joy." We're not ready to walk away from the everyday joys that delight us out here in the secular world.

That's O.K. for those who sense that special calling, but what would happen to the work and ministry of the church if all of us chose to live such an isolated life? Besides, it's not the style of life that interests most of us, and we certainly don't raise our children in hopes that they will choose such a life. Choosing the ministry or the priesthood might be the dream of a few devout parents, but being shut away in that medieval way of life? Not really.

That's close to how my twin sons felt at age thirteen when we made a brief visit to the Abbey of Gethsemane, best known because of its most famous monk, Thomas Merton. Along the wall leading to the main sanctuary, there is a gate no longer in use. It was once the entrance into an area open only to the monks. Over the granite lintel of the doorway are engraved the words, GOD ALONE.

I explained to the boys the vows that are taken by the monks, how they will spend the rest of their lives seeking God alone in a daily discipline of prayer and study, how their day begins in the middle of the night, how they will never marry, and how they observe a rule of silence, speaking only when allowed by their superiors.

"Scary," said one of boys; it was a totally undesirable existence. They didn't want the longer tour I had planned; after all, middle school kids can't take too much serious stuff.

But how dare we, as adults, sing these words, if we have no practical intention of making Jesus "our only joy"? Still, I'm not sure that such an intention is demanded by those words. If Bach's joy was exclusively in Jesus, and not also in great music, we would have none of his sublime music with which to sing praises to Jesus. My guess is that the people best qualified to help us with this question are those monks. If one of them could have talked with my boys, the monastic life might not have seemed so scary.

What they could have told them (and the rest of us also) is that the lives of monastics down through the centuries make it clear that, entering a monastery, will never allow you to escape yourself.

You can never escape your doubts, your fears, or your unanswered questions behind the walls of an abbey. You won't find all of the answers to the big questions there, nor will you forget your love of jazz, dancing, girls (or boys), fishing, or golfing. You will always be YOU! And you will still make mistakes (big ones), occasionally make a fool of yourself, and commit big sins (just ask Merton about that one).

What you will find when you enter the deeper silence that awaits each one of us in what Sister Joan Chittister calls "the monastery of heart" is that your only real Friend is Jesus. He never turns us away when others do. He never shames us when we have failed and the world condemns us. He's still there when our loved ones have died and departed. He is, truly, our only final joy.

When we know that, we live realizing that nothing "tastes good" without Jesus. Nothing is ever fun without him. No relationship is fulfilling without his presence. He's the only one who makes life complete, and the spirit of his risen presence is always with us.

When we thus discover Jesus in our interior monastery, others notice that something is different. When Canon Charles Raven went to visit a friend who had made this discovery, he wrote, "It was evident that a *third person* was there. . . . Jesus was alive and present to my friend."

Making pilgrimages back to the Abbey of Gethsemane is helpful, but I don't have to keep going back. Along every daily road, there are monastic stopping places.

After my father died, I had a dream in which he said to me, "Let the great silences feed you." Since then, it has been my experience that many secret monasteries are always awaiting.

And when I take time to enter into that holy silence, I can, indeed, sing, "Jesus, our only joy be Thou."

O Sacred Head, Now Wounded

1 O sa - cred head, now wound - ed, with grief and shame weighed down,
2 My Lord, what you did suf - fer was all for sin - ners' gain;
3 What lan - guage shall I bor - row to thank you, dear - est Friend,

now scorn - ful - ly sur - round - ed with thorns, your on - ly crown.
mine, mine was the trans - gres - sion, but yours the dead - ly pain.
for this, your dy - ing sor - row, your mer - cy with - out end?

O sa - cred head, what glo - ry and bless - ing you have known!
So here I kneel, my Sav - ior, for I de - serve your place;
Lord, make me yours for - ev - er, a loy - al ser - vant true,

Yet, though de - spised and gor - y, I claim you as my own.
look on me with your fa - vor and save me by your grace.
and let me nev - er, nev - er out - live my love for you.

4

O Sacred Head, Now Wounded

This is another hymn attributed to Bernard of Clairvaux in the twelfth century (see pp. 17–18), although some scholars argue that its author was Arnulf of Louvain of the thirteenth century.

In addition to his love of poetry that produced hymns, Bernard was one of the great preachers of his age.

Especially in light of this moving Lenten hymn, consider a few excerpts from Bernard's writings and sermons:

- How do we know that Christ has really overcome death? Precisely in that he, who did not deserve it, underwent it. . . . But what kind of justice is this, you may say, that the innocent should die for the guilty? It is not justice, but mercy.

- You will never have real mercy for the failings of another until you know and realize that you have the same failings in your soul.

- Thank you, Lord Jesus, for your kindness in uniting us to the church you so dearly love, not merely that we may be endowed with the gift of faith, but that, like brides, we may be one with you.

Bernard is a paradox to us today. He was a man of the world who defended the Crusades in vehement terms and advised kings and popes from his monastic cell. One historian has written of Bernard, "The ability of one man without political office or power to change history solely by his teaching and example is without parallel until the sixteenth century and Martin Luther."

And yet, Bernard is the same man whose fervent piety and brilliant mind tried to make the Christian faith come alive for individual Christians.

The Latin text of "O Sacred Head, Now Wounded" was translated into German by Paul Gerhardt (1607–1676). A pastor and musician, Gerhard is regarded as the most gifted and popular hymn writer in the Lutheran tradition. His life was filled with tragedy and pain, much of it caused by the Thirty Years' War.

He never found a secure job till he was forty-four; never married till four years later. His wife died after a long illness when he was unemployed. They had five children. Only one lived beyond childhood. This suffering man found solace in Christ on a cross.

The hymn text is an English translation of Gerhardt's German translation of the Latin text by one of the influential Presbyterian theologians of the nineteenth century, James Waddell Alexander. Alexander has been overshadowed in history by his father, Archibald Alexander, who was the first professor at Princeton Seminary. But James Waddell Alexander was a strong writer, preacher, and theologian in his own right, who alternated in his ministry between teaching and preaching. Like his counterparts across the Atlantic, Alexander translated a number of hymns from Greek, Latin, and German.

The historian Philip Schaff wrote that "O Sacred Head, Now Wounded" "has shown an imperishable vitality in passing from the Latin into the German, and from the German into the English, and proclaiming in three tongues, and in the name of three Confessions—the Catholic, the Lutheran, and the Reformed—with equal effect, the dying love of our Saviour, and our boundless indebtedness to Him."

Another version, widely used in Anglican and Episcopal circles, was translated by the English poet, Robert Seymour Bridges. His collection *The Yattendon Hymnal* (1899) is considered a landmark in English hymnody. The church music scholar Erik Routley said that Bridges "did more than any other person to raise English hymnody to the level of respectable literature, redeeming it from both the crudity of the eighteenth century and the conventionality of the nineteenth." Bridges was eventually named England's poet laureate.

"O Sacred Head, Now Wounded" was composed with seven parts, and each part was designed to be sung the seven days of Holy Week. The seven parts focused on different parts of Christ's body: feet, knees, hands, sides, breast, heart, and head.

The tune, Passion Chorale, was written by Hans Leo Hassler and based on a love song for singing in a bar. It is entitled in English, "My Peace of Mind Is Shattered by a Young Maiden's Charms." Using a secular tune for sacred purposes was endorsed by Luther, who said that "the devil had the best tunes."

Hassler himself is now regarded as one of the founders of German music. He was one of the first Germans to study music in Italy, and he occupied many prominent positions in Germany. He wrote a large number of works, both sacred and secular, for instrumental and choral use.

The harmonization was done by Johannes Sebastian Bach. He adored the tune and used it five times in the "St. Matthew Passion," twice in the "Christmas Oratorio," in five cantatas, and in an organ prelude.

The suffering or the passion of Christ is sometimes buried in contemporary piety and preaching, but this hymn brings it to the surface forcefully and faithfully. It is a graphic reminder that the God of love is also the God of suffering—for us and our salvation. The last verse particularly speaks of our inability to express our love for Christ in the face of God's suffering for us: "What language shall I borrow, to thank thee dearest friend"?

In the last analysis, when we stand before the cross, we are speechless before such love for us.

Meditation

Is That Our Jesus?

An acquaintance who teaches at a theological seminary was doing his best to nurture his little boy in the Christian faith, surrounding him with stories, songs, and pictures about God's love in Jesus Christ.

With such an emphasis upon the friendliness of God as manifested in the life and teaching of Jesus, it came as a shock to this five-year-old boy when, during one Lenten season, a modern artist's rendering of a thorn-crowned Christ appeared on the Sunday worship bulletin. Reacting to the grisly reality of the painting, his son asked, "Is that our Jesus?"

His early education in the faith had not prepared him for the fact that following Jesus might result in a blood-stained discipleship. Quite honestly, the little boy's question might be ours also. Does it ever occur to us that following Jesus might demand actual physical suffering? Perhaps we have almost totally dismissed such a possibility.

Several years ago it became a teenage Christian "fashion" to wear WWJD bracelets and jewelry items. Devout Christian parents embraced this fashion with great enthusiasm. What could be better than that their teenagers wear some charm that reminded them to ask, "What would Jesus do?"

One suspects that the concern of the parents was that, faced with the sexual temptations of the teen years, such Christian bangles might save their children from the allurements of the world, the flesh, and the devil. But did it occur to them that the one thing Jesus did for which he is mostly remembered was getting himself crucified?

That is certainly not the career dream that average American Christian parents have for their children. We've pretty much ruled out crucifixion as something that might happen to good Christian people.

A bronze plaque on the student center at Princeton Theological Seminary lists the names of seminary graduates who became martyrs in the proclamation of their faith. One of the most recent graduates whose discipleship led to his death was a member of my class. James Reeb, class of 1953, was brutally bludgeoned on March 7, 1965 in Selma, Alabama, dying two days later of massive brain injuries. He had gone to Selma to join protests for African American voting rights.

His murderers were acquitted, even though their attack had taken place in public. While his death raised a national outcry and hastened passage of the Voting Rights Act of 1965, the opinion of many Christians in both South and North was that such demonstrations were unnecessary and that those who engaged in them were "asking for trouble."

Of course, some well-meaning Christians fall into the trap of looking for trouble; they develop a "martyr complex" in their efforts to save the world, failing to see that such a messianic fixation is rooted in their pride of being different, in being somehow superior to ordinary Christians.

Granted all of that, could it be that our quiet dismissal of Jim Reeb's prophetic courage comes, instead, from the odd notion that the era of Christian martyrdom is long gone. It's almost like saying that Jesus and the early Christians did the dirty work so that, in our so-called Christian society, discipleship can be reduced to the practice of a non-controversial niceness.

True, in certain parts of the non-Christian world, some Christians still face persecution. But Germany was a Christian nation, so how do we account for the fact that Bonhoeffer's demonstration against a Nazi tyranny that was acceptable to many Christians resulted in his death? But that was an exception, we say; in our modern Christianized societies, such radical protest is no longer a requirement of discipleship.

It seems as though we have decided ahead of time that a thorn-crowned Christianity is no longer necessary. But our decision not to suffer goes against the history of Christian sainthood.

Beginning with Jesus, whose Palm Sunday procession into Jerusalem was a demonstration that mocked Roman imperialism as represented by the pomp of Pilate's parade that same day, those we sing about as saints have, every so often, had to suffer for the demonstration of their faith. These are painful questions, but they won't go away if we believe that the Jesus of this hymn is "our Jesus."

So here for our pondering is a poetic rendering of this hard question by Amy Carmichael, the Irish Presbyterian missionary to India.

Hast thou no scar?
No hidden scar on foot, or side, or hand?
I hear thee sung as mighty in the land,
I hear them hail thy bright ascendant star,
Hast thou no scar?
No wound? No scar?
Yet, as the Master shall the servant be,
And pierced are the feet that follow me;
But thine are whole: can he have followed far
Who has nor wound or scar?

A Mighty Fortress Is Our God

5

A Mighty Fortress Is Our God

This is perhaps the most important hymn in Protestant history. It is sometimes called "The Battle Hymn of the Reformation." It was written by Martin Luther (1483–1546), undoubtedly one of the most important figures in the history of Christianity, Germany, and indeed the Western world. His influence extended far beyond the sphere of the church to politics, economics, education, and the arts.

Luther's hymn is based on the great psalm of faith and courage, Psalm 46:

> God is our refuge and strength,
>> a very present help in trouble.
> Therefore we will not fear,
>> though the earth should change,
>> though the mountains shake in the heart of the sea;
> though its waters roar and foam,
>> though the mountains tremble with its tumult.

"A Mighty Fortress" has been enthusiastically called by historian James Moffatt "the greatest hymn of the greatest man in the greatest period in German history." Another scholar has labeled it "the national hymn of Germany." It was so much a part of Luther's life that at one point of personal trial, he sang it every day. The hymn was probably inspired by the wave of persecutions that swept over Germany in 1527 or by the Diet of Speyer in 1529, which gave rise to the term "Protestant." One early printed version of the hymn described it as "A Hymn of Comfort."

Luther himself was a musician in voice and on instruments—the flute and the lute. Through his thirty-seven hymns, he was a major factor in returning congregational singing to worship and believed strongly in the spiritual power of music. "Next to the Word of God, the noble art of music is the greatest treasure in the world," Luther wrote. "It controls our thoughts, minds, hearts, and spirits."

Luther also declared, "I am strongly persuaded that after theology, there is no art that can be placed on a level with music; for besides theology, music is the only art capable of affording peace and joy of the heart, like that induced by the study of the science of divinity. A proof of this is that the devil, the originator of sorrowful anxieties and restless troubles, flees before the sound of music almost as much as before the Word of God."

The historian Philip Schaff has written, "To Luther belongs the extraordinary merit of having given to the German people in their own tongue the Bible, the Catechism, and the hymnbook, so that God might speak directly to them in His words, and that they might directly answer Him in their songs." The poet Samuel Taylor Coleridge flatly concluded that Luther "did as much for the Reformation by his hymns as he did by his translation of the Bible."

The early English Reformer Miles Coverdale, a contemporary of Luther, provided the first English translation—a rather wooden but beautifully simple rendition. Here is part of Coverdale's translation:

Our God is a defense and towre
A good armour and good weapon
He hath been ever oure help and succore
In all the troubles we have bene in.
Therefore wyll we never drede
For any wondrous dede
By water or by londe
In hills or the sea sonde
Our god hath them al in his hond.

Today there are nearly 100 different English versions of "A Mighty Fortress," and it has been translated into more than 200 languages.

The version most of us sing was translated by Frederick Henry Hedge, Professor of Ecclesiastical History at Harvard. Hedge was a Unitarian minister and a friend of Ralph Waldo Emerson, the founder of the Transcendentalist movement. He was both a pastor and a professor throughout his ministry and known for his work introducing German writers to American readers.

The tune, "Ein' Feste Burg," was composed by Luther. It might be an adaptation of a Gregorian melody. Scholars believe it appeared first in a hymnbook published in 1529. No copy of this hymnbook exists today, but that is why our hymnbooks list the date as 1529. The earliest hymnal that includes it was published in 1531. The harmonization of the version we sing today was done by Bach, who also used it in his Cantata 80.

The tune was also used by Felix Mendelssohn in 1830 in his "Reformation Symphony," by Richard Wagner in 1871 in "Kaisersmarsch," and by a composer Giacomo Meyerbeer in 1836 in the opera "Les Huguenots." It has been widely used on public occasions, including the funeral services for President Dwight Eisenhower and Supreme Court Justice Thurgood Marshall.

In 1869, an Irish American band leader, Patrick Sarsfield Gilmore staged "A Mighty Fortress" extravaganza in Boston with a chorus of 10,000 voices and a 1,000 piece orchestra. After that, there was little doubt that the fortress was mighty.

To illustrate how things change, let me tell you a story. Several years ago I was preaching in a small Presbyterian church in West Virginia. As I drove through the town, I passed a Catholic church where Mass had just ended. The people were leaving the church, and the bell tower was playing a hymn. It was "A Mighty Fortress Is Our God." I clearly remember my astonishment and thinking, "History has happened." As a matter of fact, I learned later that "A Mighty Fortress" is in all Catholic hymnals today.

History has indeed happened. The centuries of hatred and distrust between Protestants and Roman Catholics are fortunately a part of the past, and Luther's mighty declaration now unites Christians, rather than divides them:

A mighty Fortress is our God,
A Bulwark never failing;
Our Helper He amid the flood
Of mortal ills prevailing.

Meditation

One Little Word

Some of you may know that Fred Rogers, creator of TV's *Mister Rogers' Neighborhood*, was an ordained Presbyterian minister. He had already begun his television career when he experienced his call to ministry and became a part-time student at Pittsburgh Theological Seminary.

I've often wondered if New Testament Greek was Fred's best subject, because he always wrote a few words of greeting in that ancient language on the birthday cards he sent me. Whatever may have been Fred's competence in that language in which the New Testament manuscripts were written, his favorite seminary teacher was Dr. William F. Orr, Professor of New Testament.

During Dr. Orr's final years in a nursing home, Fred and his wife, Joanne, used to visit him every Sunday after church. On one Sunday, the service had ended with Luther's hymn, with its verse,

The Prince of Darkness grim, We tremble not for him;
His rage we can endure, For lo, his doom is sure;
One little word shall fell him.

Fred was wondering about that verse, and so asked Dr. Orr what that one little word might be, that one little word that could bring down the satanic prince of darkness. Dr. Orr responded, "There is only one thing evil cannot stand and that is forgiveness."

The true gospel, the really good news, is that Jesus has already pronounced that "one little word" of forgiveness upon all of us. Yes, all of us, because we were all there on that day when the Lord of Glory was crucified. It was not only the powers of Rome and Jerusalem that were involved on that dark Friday; when the crowds shouted, "Crucify him," our voices were raised with theirs. And we continue to crucify him whenever we participate in evil systems and reject God's kingdom way of love and justice.

But at that high noon of history, when the sin of the world challenged the love of God, Jesus uttered that one word that evil cannot withstand. That pronouncement, "Father, forgive them; for they know not what they do" echoes down through all the ages and includes all of us. Many people believe that the Day of Judgment is yet to come; but I take those words literally, and believe that they signify that our day of judgment has come and gone, and that the verdict is final: we are forgiven.

God is perennially pursuing us with mercy because we could never know fully what we are doing. There are, of course, many times when we know very well what we're doing. With deliberation we fail to speak or act as God's children, hurting and abusing ourselves and others. When guilt catches up with us, aware of what we have done, we ask for and receive forgiveness—and there's no waiting! God forgives!

But the depth of God's forgiving love is manifest in the fact that we are continually being pardoned for a multitude of hurtful words and deeds of which we have no awareness whatever. One prayerbook reminds us of, "how often we do wrong from want of thought rather than from lack of love." We simply have not reached that stage of spiritual sensitivity at which we are fully aware of the true extent of our failures.

When we become even minimally aware of God's covert and constant work of forgiveness, we realize that our heavenly Father has to work around the clock just to keep up with the unrecognized sins under our own roof and in our own little neighborhood.

But everything changes in our neighborhood when we become aware of these secret showers of forgiving grace that are always pouring down from heaven. We begin to look upon our neighbors differently, as sisters and brothers of forgiven imperfection. No more pride based upon our manufactured measurements of morality or our selected standards of superiority! We're all forgiven sinners, saved by grace.

Now we speak kindlier, humbler, gentler words to one another:

> So let me draw you to the great Forgiveness,
> Not as one above who stoops to save you,
> Not as one who stands aside with counsel,
> Nay! as he who says, "I too was poisoned
> With the flowers that sting, but now, arisen,
> I am struggling up the path beside you;
> Rise and let us face these heights together."

I wonder if it was this kind of neighborhood that Fred had in mind when he showed all of us around Mister Rogers' neighborhood. Fred was not naive about the power of evil; his work with children had made him painfully aware of the awful abuse under which some children must suffer secretly.

In a few of his broadcasts, in his special way with little ones, he found words to warn them of the pervasive presence and power of evil that could afflict them. But as he spoke, he was speaking to all of us as children of God, calling all of us to make our neighborhoods sanctuaries of kindness and forgiveness.

We all have to start somewhere, so start small. Begin in your own home and in your own little neighborhood, because that is exactly where God is already present, calling you to live and speak his word of forgiveness. God will work with you, all day long, all night long—all the time!

Now Thank We All Our God

1 Now thank we all our God with heart and hands and voic - es,
2 O may this boun - teous God through all our life be near us,
3 All praise and thanks to God the Fa - ther now be giv - en,

who won - drous things has done, in whom his world re - joic - es;
with ev - er joy - ful hearts and bless - ed peace to cheer us,
the Son and Spir - it blest, who reign in high - est heav - en—

who from our moth - ers' arms has blessed us on our way
to keep us in his grace, and guide us when per - plexed,
the one e - ter - nal God, whom heaven and earth a - dore;

with count-less gifts of love, and still is ours to - day.
and free us from all ills of this world in the next.
for thus it was, is now, and shall be ev - er - more.

6

Now Thank We All Our God

This hymn is the greatest hymn of Christian courage ever written, especially when you know its history.

It was written by Martin Rinkart (1586–1649) in about 1636. Rinkart lived through one of the most vicious and savage periods of European history—the Thirty Years' War. It pitted Protestant powers against Catholic powers, and this civil war within Christianity was so devastating that entire cities disappeared from the map of Europe. Wolves returned to areas that had not seen them for centuries.

Long before we witnessed the rise of genocide and ethnic cleansing as a techniques of warfare, the Thirty Years' War brought it to Europe.

Rinkart was born in 1586, shortly after Luther's death, and died in 1649. He was a musician and Lutheran pastor for nearly all of his life in Eilenburg, a walled city in Germany.

Walled cities were advantageous because they protected the residents from the brutality of war in seventeenth-century Germany, but overcrowding also produced famine and disease and plague. The outbreak of disease was so bad that sometimes Rinkart preached burial sermons for forty to fifty people in one day.

Eventually, all the pastors in the city died, except Rinkart.

During the plague, he conducted an estimated 4,480 burials. In their home, the Rinkarts provided a safe haven for refugees. His wife died of the plague, and he came down with it but survived.

He later died, according to all reports, of sheer exhaustion.

The text comes from the Apocryphal book of Ecclesiasticus 50:22–24, which was still part of the Lutheran Bible. The reference reads in part: "Now bless the God of all, who in every way does great things." The first two stanzas are intended as a table grace— a prayer before a meal. The third stanza was added later as a Trinitarian doxology.

The translator of the hymn is the famous Catherine Winkworth (1827-1878), an Englishwoman who did more than anyone else to introduce German hymns into the worship life of English-speaking people. In fact, she translated more than 400 German texts by about 170 authors.

Many hymnals have multiple hymns that were translated by her, including "Lift Up Your Heads, Ye Mighty Gates," "If Thou but Suffer God to Guide Thee," "Jesus, Priceless Treasure," "Praise Ye the Lord, the Almighty," and "Deck Yourself, My Soul, With Gladness."

Winkworth is a powerful figure in our hymnody and an example of the impact that women played in shaping our worship life, especially since the nineteenth century. As Erik Routley once observed, women have often known the contours of the human heart and the texture of faith better than men. Another historian has written of Winkworth, "She faithfully transplanted Germany's best hymns and made them bloom with fresh beauty in their new gardens."

Winkworth translated these German hymns for her own devotional use, not because she was hired by a publisher. She was part of the evangelical movement in nineteenth-century England, a social work pioneer, and an early advocate of women's educational rights. Despite persistent sickness that kept her confined, she had many friends, including the Brontë sisters.

The tune, "Nun Danket Alle Gott," was written by Johann Crüger in 1648. Crüger was a prominent German composer and editor during the seventeenth century and contributed a substantial number of works to German sacred music. Crüger edited the most important German hymnal of the seventeenth century, which went through forty-four editions from 1644–1731.

The harmonization comes from Felix Mendelssohn's "Lobesang" or "Hymn of Praise" Symphony, written in 1840 to celebrate the 400th anniversary of printing. Mendelssohn, of course, was the famous composer who gave us the music for "Hark! The Herald Angels Sing" and the famous "Italian Symphony" and his violin concerto.

He was born into an ethnically Jewish family, and though raised as a Lutheran, he never gave up his respect and admiration for his Jewish heritage. Mendelssohn was one of the early figures in Romantic music, and though his reputation suffered during the rise of anti-Semitism in the late nineteenth and early twentieth centuries, he is now regarded as a major figure in the history of music.

Here, then, is a hymn written by a pastor in the midst of plague and death, translated by a woman out of her own piety, composed by a German musician, and harmonized by a Jewish Christian.

The creation of the hymn itself is testimony to the miracle of God's creativity and the geniuses God created. Its historical setting is an eloquent cry of faith amidst suffering—an emphatic cry of "yes!" in the face of the world saying "no." As one commentator put it, this is "thanksgiving in the midst of darkness."

In short, this is not a piece of music that simply says, "Thanks." It is a song of gratitude that there's life in the first place and that our lives belong to God. It's a prayer for Thanksgiving, to be sure, but it's also a prayer for every day.

Meditation

The Grandeur of Gratitude

W hen you close your eyes and, with your mind's inner ears
and eyes, hear this hymn, what do you hear and see?
This is a big hymn, demanding great sound in a great space, so
my imagery of this hymn carries me to a cathedral-like setting,
in which I hear a magnificent choir, accompanied by a grand
organ.

Others have had the same vision of this hymn, which ex-
plains why it was sung at both the dedication of the Cologne
Cathedral in 1882 and again at the Diamond Jubilee Service of
Queen Victoria in 1897.

But, of course, as my colleague's introduction notes, that's
not the original situation in life from which this hymn emerges.
The first two stanzas were composed as a grace to be sung at the
author's family table, and these words of thanksgiving are being
sung in the midst of terrible death and destruction.

This is a man living in the midst of scenes that offer him
almost nothing for which most of us could or would be thankful. If there is any grandeur here, then it is the grandeur of gratitude. So let's hear this hymn in another setting.

None of us knew that Mrs. Beam was "on welfare." She
was a stereotypical "little old lady" who was one of the shut-in
members of our church. I would visit her from time to time,
especially at Christmas when I would take a poinsettia plant to
her, or again at Easter when I would deliver some other springtime plant. In earlier years, she was able to walk to our church,
but now she was on my pastoral list of homebound members.

I had never known her in previous years when her husband
was working at the mill. They were the quiet, little people of
the congregation, never holding church office like the "bigger"
members, but always enriching our worship with their warmth,

simplicity, and friendliness. Before my time, and sometime after Mr. Beam's passing, Mrs. Beam had moved to a tiny rented apartment near our downtown church.

But now the entire city learned her whole story. NBC news came to our city to investigate the charges about so-called "welfare chiselers" who were, allegedly, the cause of the city's financial woes. The director of this investigative project had the idea of going to the homes of people who were on the public dole. He had somehow obtained their names and their permission to visit them, film them, and let them tell their stories, stories which, by the way, did not match the "chiseler" imagery.

I shall never forget what viewers saw and heard when the cameras arrived at the simple room in which Mrs. Beam sat by her window, looking out upon a leafless, winter tree. I had been there many times, but now the entire city was there as the reporter asked her about her life.

It was a story told many times over of how her departed husband's pension from the mill simply could not keep pace with the increased cost of living. But with cheerful words of thanksgiving, she told of how much she appreciated the small monthly check she received from the Welfare Department, and of how it provided her with a warm and safe place to live. Most of all, she was thankful for her window at which she could sit watching the little birds in the tree.

As she spoke, I remembered the words of Jesus, "Look at the birds of the air; they neither sow nor reap nor gather into barns, and yet your heavenly Father feeds them." What a scene! We were all being taken into a grand sanctuary on the evening of that television special. We were all witnessing the grandeur of gratitude!

What a stark contrast between the life of Mrs. Beam and that of those who build great houses, accumulate treasures on earth, and complain constantly of how difficult it is to find reliable help nowadays to clean their castles and polish their possessions, and of how many of these ingrates expect a handout!

And what a different kingdom Jesus envisioned than the kingdoms of this world! In the kingdom of God, the true bluebloods, the real royals, are those who look like Mrs. Beam, while the great ones of this present world begin to appear, more and more, as those who, all along, have been living in spiritual squalor.

Here's an exercise for your contemplation.

Waiting in an airport several decades ago, I sat with my little notebook and posed these questions to myself: "What if I end up in a rented room? If somehow I lost almost everything and was reduced to the sparse lifestyle of Mrs. Beam, what would I absolutely need to eke out a life of minimal happiness?"

It was not an easy task to make that frugal list. Of course, I needed my books—but how many? And I would need my computer, assuming, of course, that I could afford its upkeep, service, and replacement. And what about transportation? And then also, and also, and also! It became quite obvious that I needed more room, but I was already far exceeding the size of Mrs. Beam's humble digs.

So try making your own list today, and as you encounter your own problem of cramming all of your absolutely necessary stuff into an impossibly small space, then ask yourself the real question.

Could I be joyfully thankful, as was Martin Rinkart, amidst a scene of death and desolation? Could I ever hope to learn the grandeur of gratitude? And by the way, as you make your list, don't forget to include that utterly simple gift of a window, out of which you can look at the birds of the air.

When I Survey
the Wondrous Cross

1 When I sur - vey the won - drous cross on which the
2 For - bid it, Lord, that I should boast save in the
3 See, from his head, his hands, his feet, sor - row and
4 Were the whole realm of na - ture mine, that were a

Prince of glo - ry died, my rich - est gain I
death of Christ, my God! All the vain things that
love flow min - gled down. Did e'er such love and
pres - ent far too small. Love so a - maz - ing,

count but loss, and pour con - tempt on all my pride.
charm me most, I sac - ri - fice them through his blood.
sor - row meet, or thorns com - pose so rich a crown?
so di - vine, de - mands my soul, my life, my all.

7

When I Survey
the Wondrous Cross

We now turn to three hymns by Isaac Watts, who was born in 1674 and died in 1748. He is often called "the father of English hymnody." With Charles Wesley, who succeeded him in time, he launched the golden age of English hymnody.

To begin, a word of background about the times in which Watts did his work.

Until Watts, there was very little English hymnody. Because of the influence of English Puritans and Scotch Presbyterians, people sang Psalms. Then came Watts, who wrote hymns.

A huge and violent argument broke out.

On the one hand, the Psalm singers said that the only thing people should sing is the words of the Bible—specifically the Psalms.

On the other hand, Watts and others said that if you only sang the Psalms, you could not sing about Christ and the truth of the New Testament.

Both sides had a point. But the argument and the fight were sometimes vicious and certainly prolonged. It lasted nearly a half century. It's striking that about every fifty to one hundred years, there is a fight about music in the church. We saw it again in the nineteenth century when gospel hymns were introduced and then in the late twentieth and early twenty-first century with the rise of "contemporary Christian worship."

Basically, Watts and the hymn singers won the fight—decisively. The tradition of psalm singing was essentially obliterated from much of English-speaking worship, except in Scotland.

To give you an idea of how bitter this fight was, even in America, consider the case of the Reverend Adam Rankin. In 1789 (more than fifty years after Watts's death), Reverend Rankin rode on horseback from his congregation in Kentucky to the first General Assembly of the Presbyterian Church in the United States of America.

He pleaded with his fellow Presbyterians "to refuse to allow the great and pernicious error of adopting the use of Watts' hymns in public worship in preference to Rouse's versifications of the Psalms of David." The General Assembly listened and, in a model of Christian charity, encouraged him to be kind to those who disagreed and to cease in disturbing the peace of the church on the issue of hymns.

Watts's life captures the monumental shift in English-speaking worship. He was born into a Non-Conformist or Congregationalist family, and his father was a leading deacon. He was the first of nine children and precocious from the start. He loved words and language. He began the study of Latin at the age of four, the study of Greek when he was nine, French at eleven, and Hebrew at thirteen.

He also loved to make words rhyme, even in everyday conversation. When he was caught with his eyes open during family prayers, he replied,

> A little mouse for want of stairs
> ran up a rope to say its prayers.

This annoyed his father, who spanked him and warned him to stop rhyming. The young Isaac reportedly replied,

> Oh, father, do some pity take,
> And I will no more verses make.

When he was a teenager, Watts complained to his father about the boring and monotonous way the congregation sang Psalms. He said people sang with "dull indifference" and "a negligent and thoughtless air." His father shot back, "All right, young man, you give us something better."

And so, he did. That same night, the congregation sang a new hymn by Watts, and here is the first stanza:

Behold the glories of the Lamb
Amidst His Father's throne;
Prepare new honours for His Name
And songs before unknown.

During his lifetime he wrote about 750 hymns—"songs before unknown." Many hymnals are studded with Watts's hymns, including the three in this book: "When I Survey the Wondrous Cross," "Jesus Shall Reign Where E'er the Sun," and "Our God, Our Help in Ages Past."

But there's much more from Watts's lyric genius: "Joy to the World," "Come, Holy Spirit, Heavenly Dove," "My Shepherd Will Supply My Need," "From All That Dwell Below the Skies," "I Sing the Mighty Power of God," etc.

Watts was also a prodigious scholar who produced sixty tomes of theology and philosophy, including a widely used textbook in logic, entitled *Logic, or the Right Use of Reason in the Enquiry After Truth With a Variety of Rules to Guard Against Error in the Affairs of Religion and Human Life as well as in the Sciences.* Despite the long title, Watts's treatise was a required text at Oxford University and went through twenty editions.

There are at least two features of Watts's life that bear on his magnificent production of hymns.

First, he never married. One woman, Elizabeth Singer, fell in love with his hymns. You might say she met him over the Internet, but when she met him she was shocked. He was, she said, "only five feet tall, with a sallow face, hooked nose, prominent cheek bones, small eyes, and deathlike color." She quickly refused his matrimonial proposal, saying, "I like the jewel, but not the setting." That was as close as Watts ever came to marrying someone. His heart was poured into his hymns.

Second, he was a sickly man, and his health was expended in his writing. Though ordained as a Congregationalist minister, his health failed early in his ministry. Fortunately, he was befriended by the Lord Mayor of London, Sir Thomas Abney and his wife Lady Abney, with whom he stayed for thirty-six years until his death. When asked about the amazing duration of the stay of their distinguished guest, Lady Abney replied simply, "It was the shortest visit a friend ever paid a friend."

Now for three hymns by Isaac Watts. The first is "When I Survey the Wondrous Cross," described by the nineteenth-century literary critic, Matthew Arnold (and undoubtedly others), as "the greatest hymn in the English language." Arnold heard the hymn for the first time on the last Sunday of his life and repeated the third stanza just before he died.

Charles Wesley, who was no mean hymn writer himself and far outpaced Watts in hymn production, reportedly said he would give up all his hymns to have written this one.

The hymn is based on Galatians 6:14 (notice, it's a New Testament text): "May I never boast except in the cross of our Lord Jesus Christ."

The tune is Hamburg, composed by the great musician Lowell Mason in 1824, more than a century after Watts wrote the hymn. Mason is often called the father of American church music.

He was an American Presbyterian who served for many years as the music director of the Fifth Avenue Presbyterian Church in New York City. There he radically altered the worship life away from professional choirs, providing the music for congregational singing accompanied by organ music. Before coming to New York, he was choir director and organist at the Independent Presbyterian Church of Savannah, Georgia, and under his leadership that church created the first Sunday school for black children in America. By profession, he was a banker.

Mason is remembered chiefly for integrating into his hymn tunes the music of European classical composers and emphasizing congregational singing. The work of American composers largely fell by the wayside for a while, and yet the idea that congregations provide most of the music in worship prevailed in Protestantism until the arrival of contemporary Christian music performed by "worship teams" and "praise teams" and accompanied by guitars, drums, and other instruments.

"When I Survey the Wondrous Cross" captures two key elements of Watts's hymns. One is the objective truth of Christian doctrine—in this case, the death of Christ as salvation for our sins. The other is the subjective truth of that doctrine—how it becomes part of our minds and hearts. This double-sidedness runs through all of Watts's hymns. You never get one without the other.

The sheer beauty of Watts's hymns is testimony to the power of God to shape something of beauty. Here was an ugly man with a crippling disease, who produced hymns of lasting beauty.

The hymns themselves capture the words of the Apostle Paul, describing his thorn in the flesh: "Three times I besought the Lord about this, that it should leave me; but he said to me 'My grace is sufficient for you, for my power is made perfect in weakness.' I will all the more gladly boast of my weaknesses, that the power of Christ may rest upon me. For the sake of Christ, then, I am content with weaknesses, insults, hardships, persecutions and calamities; for when I am weak, then I am strong." (2 Cor 12:8–10)

Watts himself summed up his goal in hymn-writing: "By reading we learn what God speaks to us in his word; but when we sing, especially unto God, our chief desire is, or should be, to speak our own hearts and our words to God."

Meditation

My All?

"Love so amazing, so divine, Demands my soul, my life, my all." Some of you will think it rather odd that, whenever I sing this hymn that ends with those words, I am *not* thinking about the cross of Jesus.

The only way in which I can sing those words in which we voice such total commitment is by remembering Harry and Anna, two gentle souls whom I came to know in my teenage years. They lived in a small neighborhood on the edge of town in a tiny matchbox-size house. It was so small that, when they hired me to paint it one summer during my college years, I finished the job in less than a week and needed only a step ladder to reach the highest places.

Harry and Anna didn't own a car; they traveled to work and church by public bus. And, of course, they were always at church. As far as I could guess, Harry had only one suit, a navy blue one that was always neatly pressed, but still a bit shiny from its high mileage. Along with a white shirt and plain black tie, this one suit was Harry's haberdashery. He certainly didn't have to waste any time deciding what to wear on any day of the week.

Anna's style was similarly simple; unlike some of us whose closets are so crammed with fashionable finery that we cannot obey Jesus' command to go into our closets to pray, there would have been plenty of extra room for prayer in Anna's closet. All I can remember of her hairdo was that her braided hair was tied neatly in back. They were plain, to say the least, and could easily have made a transition into an Amish way of life.

As "out of it" as their way of life may have seemed to the rest of us, many young people counted on them for sound advice and support. Once in a time of deep depression, I turned to them for counsel because there was something honest and trustworthy about their unadorned and uncomplicated lifestyle.

Then, all of a sudden, they had a car, an unstylish used car, but a car nonetheless, and this was a surprise. But they needed a car now because they had provided the funding for the purchase of a summer camp for children. The camp was located in the countryside, inaccessible by public bus. Like their own lives, it was a simple place, once used for persons with tuberculosis.

I spent an entire summer there as a camp counselor in its early days, and it is still in operation today. And then, suddenly again it seemed, after a few years, they were gone. They had decided, in their remaining years after Harry's retirement, to live out their faith as teachers in Afghanistan from which, after nine years, they returned home for Anna's final months of life.

They chose to live as they did; they didn't have to do so. Long after they had passed away, the church treasurer, my father-in-law, confided in me the secret of their lives—and I think it's time to make it known.

Early in their marriage, maybe because they had not been blessed with children, they decided to live by (what I would describe as) a reverse tithe. They had decided to live upon 10 percent of their income and devote the remaining 90 percent to the Lord's work. My father-in-law knew this because the IRS had audited their tax returns frequently, suspecting that people who lived as they did were either liars or religious fanatics.

Of course, many of us could not live the way they did. It would be difficult to raise children, especially teenagers, while following such a way of life. And, of course, many of us are engaged in businesses or professions in which just one suit or one dress would never suffice. And of course, of course, of course . . . we have all kinds of good reasons and excuses for living the way we do.

It's tempting for a preacher to go into a "rant" about the way we misuse Isaac Watts's hymn as the closing hymn on Stewardship Sunday, singing about "giving our all," following a sermon in which we have preached our pitch for paltry percentage increases in giving.

But I'm weary of such ranting. Instead, when we sing this hymn, I choose to remember Harry and Anna. However severe and simple their lives may have been, they were two of most radiantly happy people I have ever known.

True, Jesus was the only one who gave his all; however, the world has been changed mostly by those few rare saints who have, at least, made some heroic attempt to climb all the way up the steep hill of Calvary with him.

Jesus Shall Reign

1 Je - sus shall reign wher - e'er the sun does its suc -
2 To him shall end - less prayer be made, and prais - es
3 Peo - ple and realms of ev - ery tongue dwell on his
4 Bless - ings a - bound wher - e'er he reigns: the pris -oners
5 Let ev - ery crea - ture rise and bring the high - est

ces - sive jour - neys run, his king - dom stretch from
throng to crown his head. His name like sweet per -
love with sweet - est song, and in - fant voic - es
leap to lose their chains, the wea - ry find e -
hon - ors to our King, an - gels des - cend with

shore to shore, till moons shall wax and wane no more.
fume shall rise with ev - ery morn - ing sac - ri - fice.
shall pro - claim their ear - ly bless - ings on his name.
ter - nal rest, and all who suf - fer want are blest.
songs a - gain, and earth re - peat the loud a - men.

8

Jesus Shall Reign Where'er the Sun

Despite his incredible gift for writing hymns, Isaac Watts was hardly one to abandon entirely the use of the Psalms in worship. In 1719 he published a collection whose title captures the theme of his hymns in it. It was entitled *Psalms of David, Imitated in the Language of the New Testament*.

The hymnbook, he said, gave "an evangelic turn to the Hebrew sense" and was designed to "accommodate the book of Psalms to Christian worship." In other words, these were hymns that didn't provide new versifications of the Psalms. Instead, these were hymns that imitated the Psalms.

The glorious tune for this hymn, Duke Street, is credited to John Hatton, about whom little is known except that he was an English Presbyterian who lived in the village of St. Helen's on Duke Street. He died in 1797.

"Jesus Shall Reign" comes from the second part of Psalm 72 with the subtitle "Christ's Kingdom Among the Gentiles." Some may react negatively to this implicit division of the world into "the saved" and "the Gentiles," but Watts's hymn captures perfectly the missionary impulse that was barely evident during his lifetime but which became a defining mark of western Christianity during the nineteenth century. Indeed, "Jesus Shall Reign" is often identified as the finest missionary hymn ever written.

It became an unofficial hymn for the missionary movement, which had an enormous impact in making Christianity a world religion for the first time in 2,000 years. For example, by the early twenty-first century there were nearly twice as many

Christians in Asia as in North America and almost three times as many Christians in Africa than in the United States.

By the end of the twentieth century, the numerical strength of the Christian faith had dramatically moved away from the Western world to the Southern and Eastern hemispheres, largely because of the evangelistic activities of the indigenous churches. And yet, the gospel was planted by men and women who were Western missionaries, and much of the educational and medical programs in these areas are due in no small measure to the work of those ambassadors for Christ.

Pay special attention then to the fourth stanza:

> Blessings abound where e'er he reigns;
> The prisoners leap to lose their chains,
> The weary find eternal rest,
> And all who suffer want are blessed.

Today, when so many are in poverty, so many suffer from disease or famine, and so many afflicted in spirit, let us sing with conviction that "all who suffer want are blessed."

Meditation

Hopeful About Everybody

There have been great changes since Isaac Watts wrote this hymn that "became the unofficial hymn of the missionary movement." The goal of saving souls accomplished much more than was first envisioned by those early missionaries who made heroic sacrifices lest even "one soul should perish, lost in shades of night."

Those early heralds of the good news accomplished far more than they could have realized. Schools, hospitals, orphanages, and literacy were just a few of the blessings that came to "abound where'er He reigns." Even though their scope was narrow by today's ecumenical emphases, within it they were magnificent.

They were sowing the seeds that moved the focus of the church's mission from conversion to compassion. And from this widening focus, we can learn a lesson of tremendous personal significance for our daily lives. Whenever we remember throughout every ordinary day that Jesus shall reign, we need to recall that the victory of God's kingdom has *already* been achieved.

From my boyhood days I remember General Douglas MacArthur's dramatic radio broadcast to the Filipino people a few minutes after he and his troops had landed on the island of Leyte on October 29, 1944. His words, "I have returned" referred to the pledge ("I shall return") he had made in 1942 when he had been ordered to leave his command post in the Philippines and retreat to Australia. But now, the march toward victory had begun.

But Jesus has also landed, and his landing, his announcement that the kingdom of God is at hand, is without a breath of triumphalism and in an entirely peaceful spirit. Our dramatic announcement is that the King's Son has landed to reclaim his Father's lands and people. God's invasion has begun; Jesus is peacefully invading every human life.

Do you believe that? If you do, it will change the entire spirit with which you meet everyone on every day of your life.

It will not mean that we live with the smug interior assurance that we're right and they're wrong. We do not engage with others, saying within ourselves, "You just wait; you'll have your comeuppance when Jesus returns."

That's not the spirit that rules our relationships with others when we sing, "Jesus Shall Reign." Neither does it mean that we live with the guarantee that our theology, our denomination, or even that Christianity will win.

Let us be clear about that. Christianity is the organized institutional religion that has sought to carry the message and mission of Jesus into the world. But Christianity is not Jesus. And there have always been persons of good faith who, without becoming Christians, have believed in Jesus' way of life—Gandhi, for example. So when we say that Jesus shall reign, we are not saying that the Christian church will win out and that everyone will convert to our faith.

What we are saying is that "every knee shall bow, and every tongue confess that Jesus Christ is Lord," which is to acknowledge that Jesus' life of love, peace, and compassion will be acknowledged as the goal of all human life. We don't know how the millions of the world's peoples will make their own unique expressions of their love for Jesus, but we know that Jesus will never turn anyone away who seeks to follow his way of life.

Frank Laubach (1884–1970) said it best. Here was a missionary who embodied the changing mission emphasis from conversion to compassion. There are probably more people on the face of the earth today who can read and enjoy the blessings of literacy because of his world literacy campaign.

A different kind of invasion began in 1915 when Frank Laubach and his wife arrived in the Philippines. His greatest challenge was that of somehow reaching the Muslim Moros on the island of Mindanao, a people who were virtually inaccessible to approach by a Christian missionary. However, he came finally to the realization that his mission was not about religion but about life.

In his diary on March 9, 1930, he wrote, "I must confront these Moros with a divine love which will speak Christ to them though I never use his name. . . . What right then have I or any other person to come here and change the name of these people from Muslim to Christian, unless I lead them to a life fuller of God than they have now? Clearly, clearly, my job here is not to go to the town plaza and make proselytes, it is to *live* wrapped in God, trembling to his thoughts, burning with his passion."

I still remember the night when I first heard Laubach speak and talk of missions in this deeply living sense. I still have the little booklet of his letters I picked up that night, and I still have the letter he wrote to me six weeks before his death in which he closed by saying, "God give you a tremendous fire of the Spirit."

It was his understanding of the Spirit's working in every life that gave new hope to my life and ministry because I know that Jesus is somehow reigning and working in every life. I am hopeful about everyone I ever meet. However impossible they may seem (even if they look like the enemies of Jesus), I know that they are precious to Jesus and that he will never give up on them.

It's a great way to live. It's the only way to live, because the lights of home, our eternal home, will always be burning until we all come home.

Our God, Our Help in Ages Past

1 Our God, our help in a - ges past, our hope for years to come,
2 Un - der the sha - dow of your throne your saints have dwelt se - cure;
3 Be - fore the hills in or - der stood, or earth re - ceived her frame,
4 A thou - sand a - ges in your sight are like an eve - ning gone,
5 Time, like an e - ver rol - ling stream, bears all of us a - way,
6 Our God, our help in a - ges past, our hope for years to come,

our shel - ter from the stor - my blast, and our e - ter - nal home.
suf - fi - cient is your arm a - lone, and our de - fense is sure.
from e - ver - las - ting you are God, to end - less years the same.
short as the watch that ends the night be - fore the ri - sing sun.
we fly, for - got - ten, as a dream dies at the op - ening day.
be now our guard while life shall last, and our e - ter - nal home.

9

Our God, Our Help in Ages Past

This is another Watts hymn based on a Psalm, in this case the first five verses of Psalm 90. That is largely a psalm of lament, but Watts turned it into one of the most eloquent and beautiful expressions of God's sovereignty and power in the face of human weakness and distress.

John Wesley changed the hymn to "O God, Our Help in Ages Past," but most hymnals use the original from Watts: "Our God, Our Help in Ages Past." In the name of inclusiveness, some contemporary hymnals change the fourth stanza to read "soon bears us all away" from "bears all its sons away."

The tune, St. Anne, is thought to be the work of William Croft. It was published anonymously in a book of psalms in 1708, but it is believed to be Croft's composition. The name of the tune comes from St. Anne's Church in Soho, where Croft was organist. He was one of the most distinguished musicians of his day, and when he died, he was buried at Westminster Abbey with this epitaph: "Having resided among mortals for fifty years, behaving with the utmost candor . . . he departed to the heavenly choir . . . that being near, he might add to the concert of angels his own Hallelujah."

St. Anne radiates musical power and has helped make the hymn famous. Handel used the tune in an anthem, "O Praise the Lord." Bach's "Fugue in E-flat Major" incorporates the tune, but it's not clear whether he actually used the tune or, having heard it, adapted it in a fugal form. Ralph Vaughn Williams relied upon St. Anne for an anthem, "Lord, Thou Hast Been Our Refuge." The bells of St. Clement's Church in London play it every day.

One music scholar has concluded about St. Anne, "As a musical setting for Watts' words . . . will never be superseded. The words and music fit as hand in glove."

The immediate setting for Watts's writing "Our God, Our Help in Ages Past" was the political anxiety about who would succeed Queen Ann upon her death in 1714. But, according to one author, it became "the great ceremonial hymn of the English nation."

It was sung at Robert Browning's funeral and at the funeral service for Winston Churchill at St. Paul's Cathedral in London in 1965. People have described it as "the greatest" of all of Watts' hymns, as "one of the greatest hymns of our language," "the second national anthem of England," and as simply "a perfect hymn."

One insight into its power came from an author who said, "It swells like the ocean: it sobs out the grief of centuries."

Watts provided a subtitle: "Man Frail, and God Eternal." All of us know the storms of life—in one degree or another. Ernest Hemingway wrote, "The world breaks everyone, and afterward many are strong at the broken places."

And many are strong because of God's strength. As we sing Watts's beautiful hymn, let us also think with freshness and hope about God's power to heal us and make us whole:

> Be Thou our guard while life shall last
> And our eternal home.

Meditation

No Place Else to Go

In my seminary days, my first student weekend pastorate was in a small, blue-collar congregation of seventy-eight members.

I would arrive on Friday night, make house calls on Saturday, preach twice on Sunday, and then head back to Princeton.

For housing, I was provided with a bedroom in the tiny bungalow of Ada Zerbe, a young widow who was raising a teenage daughter and a seven-year old boy named Malcolm. It was not a spacious arrangement, but Ada was a good mother, doing her best for her children, following the shooting death of her husband in a gas station robbery. She had even gone to the trial of her husband's murderer, pleading that he not be given the death sentence. That's the kind of merciful soul she was.

I've never forgotten a story she told me about Malcolm. Once when he was five years old, he had become very angry with his mother and had decided to leave home. As Malcolm packed his little suitcase for his journey to the wide world out there, Ada told him that she would certainly be missing him but would always be awaiting his return.

Unmoved by his mother's patience, Malcolm departed through the kitchen door, saying a brief goodbye to his mother and the family cat that was perched on the window sill.

Ada watched from the front window as Malcolm walked to the corner, where he sat down on his suitcase to contemplate his travel plans. Of course, there was nowhere he could go. This was a post-World War II subdivision, far from the city, with no bus service.

After about thirty minutes, Malcolm picked up his suitcase and trudged homeward in defeat. Entering the kitchen door, to announce his arrival, he glanced about and said, "I see you still have the same old cat."

God is *our* eternal home. It is only in God's presence that we will ever, finally, be at home. We can keep on running away but, in the end, we have no place else to go.

Many years later, in a seminar for pastors taught by a distinguished preacher, our leader was commenting upon the story of the rich young man who, refusing Jesus' invitation to

discipleship, "went away grieving, for he had many possessions" (Mark 10:22). How interesting that Jesus did not chase
after him, or assign one of his disciples the task of keeping in
touch with such a promising prospect, which is what most successful modern pastors would have done.

It was as though Jesus was saying, "Let him go for now;
sooner or later he'll be back, because there's no place else to go."

I have always connected the ending of Mark's account with
another story that Jesus told, the so-called story of the prodigal
son—or better termed, the story of the prodigal *sons*.

We're never told how the story ends. As the curtain closes,
the father is outside the house, standing in the darkness with
the pouting elder brother, who is refusing to join the welcome
home party for his younger brother. Did that sulking brother
ever accept the father's invitation to come home to the party?
We don't know.

As the curtain closes, all we see is that the father is still out
there in the darkness with the son who hadn't decided to return
to his only home. That is why, I suspect, Jesus didn't chase after the rich young man. He knew that our heavenly Father will
never give up until all of us have come home to the only home
we can ever have.

May God give us patience and hope for all of those who
have not yet come home. Our loving God isn't just watching
from the front window as we try to run away. Our heavenly
Father stands with us on that street corner, and will be there
with us until we trudge home to be welcomed by the friendly
faces of our heavenly family—and that same old cat.

O for a Thousand Tongues to Sing

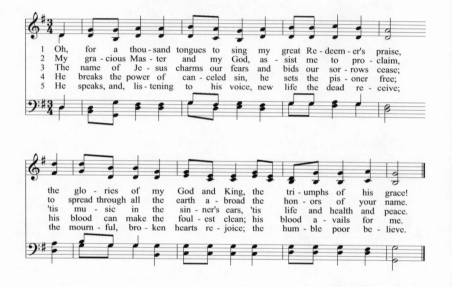

1 Oh, for a thou-sand tongues to sing my great Re-deem-er's praise,
2 My gra-cious Mas-ter and my God, as-sist me to pro-claim,
3 The name of Je-sus charms our fears and bids our sor-rows cease;
4 He breaks the power of can-celed sin, he sets the pis-oner free;
5 He speaks, and, lis-tening to his voice, new life the dead re-ceive;

the glo-ries of my God and King, the tri-umphs of his grace!
to spread through all the earth a-broad the hon-ors of your name.
'tis mu-sic in the sin-ner's ears, 'tis life and health and peace.
his blood can make the foul-est clean; his blood a-vails for me.
the mourn-ful, bro-ken hearts re-joice; the hum-ble poor be-lieve.

10

O for a Thousand Tongues to Sing

Charles Wesley, perhaps forever known as the brother of John Wesley, lived from 1707 to 1788. His extraordinary musical productivity built upon the foundation laid by Watts, but he multiplied it many-fold. During his lifetime, he composed more than 6,500 hymns and published sixty-four different hymnbooks.

Some of his hymns are the greatest in the history of the church, and he is rightly called "the sweet Bard of Methodism."

Henry Ward Beecher, the so called "prince of the Victorian pulpit," once said, "I would rather have written that hymn of Wesley's, 'Jesus, Lover of My Soul,' than to have the fame of all the kings that ever sat on the earth." The great hymnologist, John Julian, concluded that "perhaps, taking quantity and quality into consideration [Charles Wesley was] the greatest hymnwriter of all ages."

The two Wesleys—John and Charles—started a movement, Methodism, that has transformed Protestantism and indeed all of Christianity throughout the world.

To comprehend the Wesleys, you need to understand their mother, Susanna Wesley, one of the most remarkable women in church history. Susanna Wesley was a woman of prodigious piety and extraordinary order. Their father, Samuel, was a somewhat prickly rector in the Church of England, but their mother was a woman of beauty, learning, efficiency, and piety.

She gave birth to nineteen children, only ten of whom lived beyond infancy. She educated all her children—not simply in the three R's but also in Latin, Greek, history, literature, and of course religion. She set aside one evening a week for each of the children to discuss their educational and spiritual development.

When John and Charles left for Oxford, they continued this disciplined approach to the Christian life. Their small group meetings of students focused on concentrated study and training each other in the spiritual life, and so they were derisively called "Methodists" because of their "methods."

Like Watts, Charles was attacked during his lifetime for abandoning Psalm singing in favor of hymn singing, but he was also criticized for his theology, which placed an emphasis on the human will in assenting to God's love and offer of salvation. This position, known as Arminianism, was an issue for all the Methodists and still strikes a tension between Methodism and some other traditions.

Watts was more of a Calvinist and wrote hymns that were objective and yet true. Wesley was more of an Arminian and wrote hymns that were subjective and yet true. One spoke more to the head, the other spoke more to the heart.

Both John and Charles Wesley remained ordained priests in the Church of England throughout their lives—despite deep strains between them and most of the rest of the Church of England. John was the itinerant minister. His ministry lasted for fifty years—into his eighties—and he traveled more than 250,000 miles and preached 40,000 to 50,000 sermons. John was the famous Methodist.

Like John, Charles also itinerated as a preacher, but because of John's public fame, Charles is sometimes called "the forgotten Methodist." Yet anyone who sings hymns knows Charles Wesley.

He gave the ardor and spirit to Methodism and is responsible for the early Methodists to be described sarcastically as those "singing Methodists." Today, few remember John Wesley's theology, but everyone remembers Charles Wesley's hymns.

Charles worked hard writing his hymns for the Methodists, often composing his hymns on horseback. One day when his horse fell on him and he sprained his wrist, he complained that the horse had "spoiled my hymn writing for that day."

He also sought with persistence the right tunes to go with his poetry. The effort paid off. One contemporary wrote about the early Methodist gatherings: "Never did I hear such praying or such singing. Their singing was not only the most harmonious and delightful I ever heard, but they sang 'lustily and with a good courage.' . . . If there be such a thing as heavenly music upon earth I heard it there."

Another contemporary said, "The song of the Methodists is the most beautiful I ever heard. . . . They sing in a proper way, with devotion, serene mind, and charm."

The *London Quarterly* concluded that Charles Wesley "was, perhaps, the most gifted minstrel of the modern Church."

In contemporary hymnals, Charles Wesley's genius is always bountifully represented by such hymns as "Come, Thou Long Expected Jesus," "Hark, the Herald Angels Sing," "Jesus Christ is Risen Today," "Rejoice, the Lord Is King," "Christ the Lord Is Risen Today," "Love Divine All Love's Excelling," "Come, Thou Almighty King," and others.

"O for a Thousand Tongues to Sing" is the premier hymn of Methodism and has nearly always been hymn number one in a Methodist hymnal.

It was written to celebrate the first anniversary of Charles Wesley's conversion on May 28, 1738.

Here is the setting for his acceptance of Christ. Charles was seriously ill and suffering from a bout of pleurisy while he and John were studying with the Moravian Peter Böhler in London. Besides his poor physical health, Charles was plagued with spiritual doubts, even though he had already been ordained in the Church of England.

A group of Christians came to him, read him passages from the Bible, and he was greatly comforted. He found himself at peace with God. Shortly after that, John Wesley had his famous Aldersgate experience in which he said his heart was "strangely warmed."

When the two brothers wrote to their mother about their conversions, she replied, "I heartily rejoice that you have attained to a strong and lively hope in God's mercy through Christ. Not that I can think that you were without saving faith before, but it is one thing to have faith, and another thing to be sensible we have it."

One immediate consequence of Charles' conversion was his rejection of alcohol. He wrote, "I was amazed to find my old enemy, intemperance, so suddenly subdued, that I almost forgot I was ever in bondage to him."

A year after his conversion, Charles sat down to write a hymn to remember the occasion of his rebirth in Christ, which he subtitled "For the Anniversary Day of One's Conversion." Originally, the hymn had eighteen stanzas, only four of which we sing today. The seventh stanza is actually the first stanza, "O For a Thousand Tongues to Sing." It recalls the words of Peter Böhler himself, who said, "Had I a thousand tongues I would praise Him with them all."

The tune is Azmon, composed by a nineteenth-century German musician, Carl G. Gläser (1784–1829), who started out studying law but eventually turned to music. In addition to teaching music and conducting choirs, he wrote various motets, chorales, and instrumental music and managed his own music store. The tune was arranged by the great Lowell Mason (see pp. 52–53), who also gave it the name of Azmon, which is the Hebrew word for "fortress."

As you sing, pay special attention to the third stanza: "Christ breaks the power of reigning sin, And sets the prisoner free." Much of the early work of the Methodists in England focused on bringing the gospel to people in prison, and these words are a symbol of a great and needed ministry of his day and our own.

Today they can also be sung with keen awareness of the physical and emotional bondage that scars the lives of people, near at home and around the world.

Charles Wesley suffered from illness during his entire life, but he kept preaching and writing. On his death bed, he dictated a hymn of praise for his wife.

As you study and sing this hymn, you can feel the joy of Charles as he looks back on the moment when God's love in Christ became especially real to him in his sickness and weakness. Perhaps you can use this hymn to recall the moment or moments in your own life where you believed like this:

> Jesus, the name that charms our fears,
> That bids our sorrows cease;
> 'Tis music in the sinner's ears,
> 'Tis life, and health, and peace.

Meditation

O for Just One Tongue to Sing!

I don't think I have enough physical or mental energy to be a true Wesleyan. The boundless energy of both Charles and John Wesley convince me that Calvinism was a better choice for me. With so much to be done to spread "the honors of Thy name," I just can't do it all and need to leave most of it to my Calvinist God's doing.

It is simply exhausting to think of Susanna Wesley's tireless tutelage of her children, and then of Charles Wesley's 6,500 hymns and John Wesley's 40,000 to 50,000 sermons.

According to one of my students who was writing his doctoral thesis upon a particular aspect of Wesley's theology, John Wesley was so busy with his itinerant ministry that he didn't even make it to his wife's funeral! Whether or not that's true, some evidence indicates that such might have been the case.

When, at age eighteen, I was a still a newly converted Christian, some devout neighbors drove me to a Methodist "holiness" college in the hope that I might choose to enroll there. During my four days there, I attended every evening meeting of the Holiness Emphasis Week that was in progress, and also found time to read John Wesley's treatise on Christian perfection.

Even though I didn't end up at that college, the depth of faculty and student devotion to the living of a devout and holy life left its mark upon me. I have never ceased to admire the sheer goodness of certain Methodist pastors whom I have met along the way of my pilgrimage.

And now, many decades later, I continue to find it inspiring that John Wesley thought of the entire world as his parish. Both John and Charles were priests of the Church of England, but neither felt limited by the parochial bounds of the local church.

Every so often, I read John Wesley's formula for faithful discipleship, "Do all the good you can, by all the means you can, in all the ways you can, in all the places you can, at all the times you can, to all the people you can, as long as you can." Whew! What commitment!

But as I sing this number one hymn of Methodism, I have a curiously adverse reaction: a more modest "methodism" must be my manner of life.

For starters, I have only one tongue, and I've always found it quite a challenge to control just that one tongue. For that matter, most of the damage that I've done in the world started with my tongue.

Little wonder that the Letter of James observes that this smallest member of our body starts all kinds of fires; indeed, is so unruly that "no one can tame the tongue" (3:8). The same epistle enjoins me instead to "be quick to listen, slow to speak, slow to anger" (1:19).

As soon as I finish singing this hymn, I need to sit down quietly and remember Pascal's injunction, "We must keep silent as much as possible and talk with ourselves only of God, whom we know to be true." In fact, I sometimes want to ask Charles Wesley, "Why should I desire a thousand tongues when I can't even control one?"

If I can win just that one battle, then I must focus also upon something more modest than spreading my gospel message "through all the earth abroad." Just my own neighborhood of less than 100 homes will be a good starting point, and I know that the lives of my neighbors, as the children of God, are as precious to God as those far away.

It may not be a great missionary adventure to carry on a ministry of quiet friendship to those so close by, but the worry and wonder of their seemingly little lives is of eternal importance to God. Indeed, beginning from some such small neighborhood, some saints have moved the entire world.

One of them wrote, "Do your little bit of good where you are; it's those little bits of good put together that overwhelm the world." Those are the words of Archbishop Desmond Tutu, and this one faithful man has truly overwhelmed the world by bringing truth and reconciliation to South Africa, instead of what was predicted to be a literal bloodbath.

But then, I have one other tiny tool of ministry, the power of which the Wesleys could not have dreamed in their wildest imagination: I have my three-pound laptop from which I can reach around the world in ministry. Yes, the world is my parish too!

From the tiny scriptorium in which I write, watching little children playing in the neighborhood park, I can be in prayerful Internet conversation with my young friend, Pat, as he struggles with inoperable cancer hundreds of miles away. Far to the north near Chicago, I can be working with Karen, a gifted young preacher, as I stand beside her as a mentor in reviewing her sermons every week. Then there's Jeff, a retired Methodist pastor, whose simplicity, decency, and holiness of life are a credit to the Wesleyan tradition; Jeff and I can be in brotherly contact by email. And there are many more whose stories I cannot take time to tell.

No, I don't wish for a thousand tongues! But still, the world is my parish too, and I hope that the Wesleys sometimes are looking down and rejoicing in heaven over one Calvinist who, in his own way, is struggling up the steep slope of holiness, glad for their hymns and words that speak to all of us, even today.

Christ the Lord Is Risen Today

1. Christ the Lord is risen to-day,__ Al - - le - lu - ia!
2. Love's re-deem-ing work is done,__ Al - - le - lu - ia!
3. Lives a-gain our glo-rious King,__ Al - - le - lu - ia!
4. Soar we now where Christ has led,__ Al - - le - lu - ia!
*5. Hail the Lord of earth and heaven, Al - - le - lu - ia!
*6. King of glo-ry, soul of bliss,__ Al - - le - lu - ia!

Earth and heaven in cho-rus say,__ Al - - le - lu - ia!
Fought the fight, the bat-tle won,__ Al - - le - lu - ia!
Where, O death, is now thy sting?__ Al - - le - lu - ia!
Fol-lowing our ex - al - ted Head,__ Al - - le - lu - ia!
Praise to thee by both be given,__ Al - - le - lu - ia!
E - ver-las-ting life is this,__ Al - - le - lu - ia!

Raise your joys and tri-umphs high, Al - - le - lu - ia!
Death in vain for-bids him rise, Al - - le - lu - ia!
Once he died our souls to save, Al - - le - lu - ia!
Made like him, like him we rise, Al - - le - lu - ia!
Thee we greet tri - um-phant now, Al - - le - lu - ia!
Thee to know, thy power to prove, Al - - le - lu - ia!

11

Christ the Lord Is Risen Today

Charles Wesley wrote this hymn for the first worship service at the Wesleyan Chapel in London, and it was composed soon after "O for a Thousand Tongues to Sing." This chapel was located on the site of an iron foundry, and so it became known to history as the Foundry Meeting House.

After Charles Wesley died, John Wesley collected some of his hymns, and curiously he did not include this one. Fortunately, subsequent editors corrected John Wesley's lapse in judgment.

This hymn is a variation of another hymn, "Jesus Christ is Risen Today." The present hymn is written entirely by Wesley, though originally with many more stanzas. The other hymn was originally a fourteenth-century Latin hymn that had been translated into English. Charles Wesley added verses to it.

"Christ the Lord Is Risen Today" is usually sung to the tunes, Easter Hymn or Llangfair. The author of Easter Hymn is unknown, but the original form of the joyous melody was entitled "The Resurrection" and appeared in the hymnbook *Lyra Davidica* in 1708. Only one copy of this collection of hymns survives in the British Museum, and Easter Hymn is the only tune from *Lyra Davidica* that is still sung today.

Easter Hymn has been the most popular arrangement for "Christ the Lord Is Risen Today," and one commentator has said, "There is probably no tune in Christendom so universally sung on any festal day as is the Eastern hymn . . . on Easter morning."

We know more about the optional tune, Llanfair. It was composed by the nineteenth-century musician Robert Williams

(1781–1821). The name comes from an impossibly long Welsh word which means: "Church of St. Mary in a hollow of white hazel near the rapid whirlpool of the Church of St. Tysillio by the red cave." Those Welsh!

Robert Williams was born blind. Although he was trained as a basket weaver, he was a gifted singer and composer who was able to transcribe a tune upon hearing it only once.

The harmonization comes from another Welshman, David Evans, a twentieth-century musician of considerable renown, both in his native Wales and in England. For most of his career he was professor of music at University College, Oxford University. He was a very popular conductor of Welsh singing festivals and died the day after he directed a chorus of 4,000 voices.

The hymn is obviously an Easter hymn, with each line punctuated by an exclamatory "Alleluia!"

As you sing, ponder anew what Christ's resurrection means for you. How has Christ's death and resurrection given you a new life? What does that mean for how you live and think and act?

Meditation

No Longer Afraid of Life

Our nine-year-old grandson, Carson, had an interesting question during Holy Week. Listening to all of the talk in church about the coming of Easter, he asked, "Does Jesus rise again every year?" Some of what he was hearing in the preparations for Easter must have seemed very real to him, so real as to suggest that, in some other realm of spiritual fantasy, Jesus was actually going to rise again.

I can't remember how we responded, but I'm guessing that we probably told him that the resurrection happened many centuries ago, and that we were simply getting ready for our annual remembrance of that great event of long ago. It would never have occurred to us to tell him that Jesus is actually rising again today—today, and every day!

Of course, as we arrive annually at our observance of Easter, it is difficult not to think about the past, about past Easter Sundays of our childhood when, perhaps, three generations of our family sat in the same pew. But now those grandparents have passed over to the other side, into that everlasting life that Easter sermons proclaim.

If that was not our experience with grandparents, then perhaps we remember the Easters when we were raising our children, how we got them ready for church in special outfits, and tried to explain to them that Easter is not about the Easter bunny, but about God's gift of eternal life, even if we did succumb to custom and gave them those Easter baskets.

Now our children are gone too, married and raising their own children and, hopefully, trying to teach their children what we attempted to teach them. What a great treasury of memory and hope we bring to church on Easter!

But these feelings about past and future Easters can lead to misunderstandings about the true meaning of Easter. We can place the meaning of Easter in the past and future, rather than in the present. We can end up believing that Easter is *something that happened to Jesus in the past* that has to do with *something good that will happen to us in the future after we die.*

However, as the New Testament records the reactions of the visitors to the empty tomb on that first Easter morning, it is rather amazing that there is no mention whatever about a future Christian hope. Instead, as the meaning of those stories is interpreted in the letters of the New Testament, the resurrection was understood as a very this-worldly, present event.

Little Carson was coming very close to the real truth expressed in Wesley's glorious hymn; the resurrection of Jesus Christ is something that is happening today. The earliest followers of Jesus believed that, in the victorious resurrection of Jesus, the God of Israel had become King of the world. God's reign (God's Kingdom) had arrived. The Roman Empire (and all other worldly empires) had lost, and God's Empire had won!

Even though many Christians in the succeeding centuries would be put to death by the Caesars and other tyrants of this world, from the first Easter and onward, the followers of the risen Jesus could say, *"We're not afraid of you any longer; you don't have the last word. Jesus Christ is risen and our God is the ruling King of the world."*

They were no longer afraid of life, no longer living in fear of what the world could do to them. As Paul wrote, "Neither death, nor life, . . . nor anything else in all creation, will be able to separate us from the love of God in Christ Jesus our Lord."

Easter is about facing life fearlessly, about being able to say that we are no longer afraid of what life can do to us, of what the future may bring, of what may happen to our career or bank account, of what our enemies may do to us or to our nation, of what dry days of boredom may do to our spirits, of what disease may do to our bodies, of what the weight and woe of aging, with loss of friends and diminishing strength, may bring. We are no longer afraid of life.

Resurrection faith is about life *before* death. On every morning (not just on Easter, and not just in church worship), we should sing in our heart of hearts, "Christ the Lord Is Risen Today" because we are no longer afraid of life. Indeed, we have important work to do on every day as we follow the risen Jesus in whatever way we are called to be some part of the building God's kingdom. Every little thing we do in this great work is going to last forever.

So I can be excited about what today will bring. If I have discovered this new, risen life in Christ, there will be new adventures for me today. If I am changed by the present power of Jesus' resurrection, the people whom I meet today can be changed in some way.

They may experience Jesus' resurrection life in me, or I may sense his risen presence in them. This is big! This is exciting! *I am no longer afraid of life.* Christ the Lord is risen *today*!

Love Divine, All Loves Excelling

1 Love di - vine, all loves ex - cel - ling, Joy of heaven to earth come down,
2 Breathe,O breathe thy lo - ving Spi - rit in - to e - very trou - bled breast;
3 Come, al - migh - ty to de - li - ver, let us all thy life re - ceive;
4 Fi - nish then thy new cre - a - tion, pure and spot - less let us be;

fix in us thy hum - ble dwel - ling, all thy faith - ful mer - cies crown.
let us all in thee in - he - rit, let us find the pro - mised rest.
sud - den - ly re - turn, and ne - ver, ne - ver - more thy tem - ples leave.
let us see thy great sal - va - tion per - fect - ly re - stored in thee:

Je - sus, thou art all com - pas - sion, pure, un - boun - ded love thou art;
Take a - way the love of sin - ning, Al - pha and O - me - ga be;
Thee we would be al - ways bles - sing, serve thee as thy hosts a - bove,
changed from glo - ry in - to glo - ry, till in heaven we take our place,

vi - sit us with thy sal - va - tion, en - ter e - very trem - bling heart.
end of faith, as its be - gin - ning, set our hearts at li - ber - ty.
pray and praise thee with - out ceas - ing, glo - ry in thy per - fect love.
till we cast our crowns be - fore thee, lost in won - der, love, and praise.

12

Love Divine, All Loves Excelling

This is often considered the greatest of all Charles Wesley's hymns. It is certainly one of his best known and one of his most popular hymns. By the end of the nineteenth century, it was used in fifteen of the seventeen hymnals surveyed by a music periodical of the time.

Today it appears almost universally in Methodist, Anglican, and ecumenical hymnbooks as well as hymnals published by the Reformed, Presbyterian, Baptist, Brethren, Lutheran, Congregationalist, Pentecostal, and Roman Catholic traditions. One survey of North American hymnals found it appeared in 1,328 hymnbooks, more than even "Amazing Grace."

In 1747 it was published in four stanzas in a book entitled, *Hymns for those that seek, and those that have Redemption in the Blood of Christ.*

This hymn, like all of Wesley's hymns, refers to many different biblical passages. Like Watts, Wesley was essentially a poet who put the Bible into verse, and he certainly knew Scripture. The biblical references for this hymn alone are from Revelation 21, John 3 and John 15, Malachi 3, 2 Corinthians 3 and 5, and 2 Peter.

The inspiration for the hymn undoubtedly came from a song in John Dryden's operatic play, *King Arthur.* Look at the words to the first stanza and listen to these words of Dryden:

> Fairest Isle, All Isles Excelling,
> Seat of Pleasures, and of Loves;
> Venus here, will choose her Dwelling,
> And forsake her Cyprian Groves.

You can see a loose Trinitarian structure to the hymn: the first stanza speaks of Christ; the second of the Holy Spirit; the third of God the Father; and the final stanza of the Trinity itself as God the creator.

Although many tunes have been used with "Love Divine, All Love's Excelling," the most popular has been Beecher. It was composed by John Zundel (1815–1882), who was born and educated in Germany but spent most of his musical career in the United States, including nearly thirty years as the organist and director of music at Henry Ward Beecher's Plymouth Congregational Church in Brooklyn. The tune is named for Zundel's renowned partner in worship.

Some hymnbooks eliminate the second stanza with its line: "Take away the love of sinning." The objection is that this is too close to the Methodist doctrine of perfection or ultimate sanctification. I believe it is right to include it. After all, what could our hearts want more than to be freed from what we desire most but which is contrary to what God wants us to be?

Meditation

Do Things Get Bigger and Better?

A former next-door neighbor returned for a visit yesterday after being away for five years. He could hardly believe how much everything had changed. The little trees we had planted were no longer little; the small bushes were now like a high wall between what had been his house and ours.

He even thought that some things had changed that hadn't changed at all. There is a tiny park next to our home, just a little corner of the neighborhood, with a circular walkway, a few picnic tables, and a jungle gym for children.

But Tom somehow remembered it as being very large. He remembered how he had enjoyed walking his dog there before going to work each day and how those morning jaunts seemed like long walks in a large park. Of course, nothing had changed; it's still the same little park.

Why do pleasant places in our past grow in memory? I once returned to the public park in the neighborhood of my childhood; I wanted to show my children the big hill where we came flying down toward the ski jumps we constructed in the winter months.

"Where's the big hill, Dad?" they asked in disbelief. I wondered if some giant earth-moving machine had taken the top off the hill. It was just a gentle rise in elevation at the north end of the park, and the big pine trees were still there as evidence that it could never have been anything other than a little hill.

Do good memories get bigger and better? More importantly, do good people get bigger and better?

My guess is that Charles Wesley must have been reading from one of Paul's Corinthian letters on the day he wrote this hymn. The final verse ends with the prayer that the work of God's new creation will be completed in us; that we will be perfectly restored, "changed from glory into glory."

It sounds very much like Paul's words (2 Cor 3:18), "But we all, with open face beholding as in a glass the glory of the Lord, are changed into the same image from glory to glory." A closer rendering might be "from one degree of glory to another."

No one can keep looking daily at the glory of God in the face of Jesus Christ without, in some way, becoming like him. And some people are doing just that; they are becoming more gloriously godlike, becoming better every day. And in that sense, they are also becoming bigger, more spiritually spacious, making more room for God in their lives, every day.

We often forget something very important about what will constitute greatness in what will finally become the kingdom of

God on earth. As we pray daily, "Thy kingdom come, thy will be done, on earth as it is in heaven," we may fail to notice that God doesn't read our newspapers as we do.

Our headlines are not necessarily catching God's attention. Our big news may not be God's big news. The big newsmakers in our world may not be the big newsmakers in the kingdom of God. What is eternally newsworthy in God's sight will probably be unnoticed and unmentioned on tonight's evening news.

The really big news in God's kingdom for today may be about some poor unknown saint on the other side of our world who, today, made an enormous sacrifice in helping one of "the least" of those who matter in God's eyes. Some unnoticed effort at goodness by which you—yes, you—struggle up the steep slope of justice and righteousness may matter more to God than anything that wins the world's passing applause.

When God's New Jerusalem finally comes down to earth from heaven "as a bride adorned for her husband," we will discover it to be the kind of holy society in which all our earthly values are turned upside down. We don't know those who will be the big people in God's kingdom, but God does!

On every day, God is watching their battles with evil, their struggles to do justice, love kindness, and walk humbly with God. Yes! As they labor, unobserved by the world, to grow from glory to glory, God is cheering and applauding! In God's eyes, they are growing both bigger and better.

Come, Thou Almighty King

1 Come, thou Al - migh - ty King, help us thy
2 Come, thou In - car - nate Word, gird on thy
3 Come, Ho - ly Com - for - ter, thy sa - cred
4 To Thee, great One in Three, e - ter - nal

name to sing, help us to praise: Fa - ther, all
migh - ty sword, our prayer at - tend: come, and thy
wit - ness bear in this glad hour: thou who al -
prai - ses be hence, e - ver - more! Thy so - vereign

glo - ri - ous, o'er all vic - to - ri - ous,
peo - ple bless, and give thy word suc - cess:
migh - ty art, now rule in ev - ery heart,
ma - je - sty may we in glo - ry see,

come and reign o - ver us, An - cient of Days.
Spi - rit of ho - li - ness, on us des - cend.
and ne'er from us de - part, Spi - rit of power.
and to e - ter - ni - ty love and a - dore!

13

Come, Thou Almighty King

This gorgeous hymn has been called "one of the brightest hymns in our language," and it is often used as the opening hymn in a worship service. It is sometimes attributed to Charles Wesley because it originally appeared in a hymnbook edited by the Wesley's colleague, George Whitefield, one of the greatest preachers in the history of the church.

However, it is unlikely that Charles Wesley wrote it since it never appeared in any of the Wesleyan hymnbooks, and it has an unusual meter that Charles Wesley never used. So, it appears that the author is anonymous.

The tune, Italian Hymn, was written by Felice de Giardini. It was published in a book entitled *A Collection of Psalm and Hymn Tunes Never Published Before.* The book was known as the Lock Collection because it was printed to benefit Lock Hospital in Hyde Park, London. The tune, however, was actually composed nineteen years earlier than the publication of this hymn, and it was designed for the British national anthem, "God Save Our Gracious King."

Giardini was an eighteenth-century Italian musician whose work included operas, violin music, and oratorios. His own instrument was the violin, which he played brilliantly, and he was well known throughout Europe. Sadly, he was not much of a success as an opera manager, and his business had huge losses while he managed the Italian Opera Company, the Haymarket Comic Opera in London, and an opera company in Moscow.

He also had a very mercurial personality; one author writes "that he spoke well of few and quarreled with many." He died in Moscow in "poverty, disappointment, and distress."

One story behind the tune and this hymn involves a congregation on Long Island during the American Revolution. When British soldiers ordered them to sing "God Save the King," the congregation responded by singing "Come, Thou Almighty King."

Please note two things about the text of this hymn.

First, it's a hymn about the Trinity. That doctrine is one of the defining characteristics of the Christian faith, and it's been widely debated from the early days of Christianity down to the twenty-first century. Despite the debate, it lies at the very heart of what it means to be a Christian—one God in three persons or manifestations or revelations. As John Wesley declared, "Tell me how it is that in this room there are three candles and but one light, and I will explain to you the mode of the divine existence." Singing "Come, Thou Almighty King" is like singing, "This is what it means to be a Christian."

Second, pay special attention to the third verse, which sings of the Holy Spirit. The last line is particularly powerful as an antidote to loneliness—which is perhaps the greatest problem of spiritual life for contemporary people. Hear it now and sing it boldly:

Thou who almighty art,
Now rule in every heart,
And ne'er from us depart,
Spirit of power.

Meditation

It's a Beautiful Day in the Neighborhood

This hymn, like nearly all hymns, is a prayer, and it's an expansion upon the first petition of the Lord's Prayer, "Thy kingdom come, Thy will be done on earth, as it is in heaven." That greatest prayer of Jesus is addressed to our heavenly Father, but this "enlarged edition" is addressed to our Triune God.

We begin, therefore, with the realization that this hymn's prayer is already being answered. God is already engaged in that for which we are asked to pray. When we offer the Lord's Prayer, we are entering into what God has already begun. God's kingdom has already "landed" on earth; the invasion has begun.

In the life, death, and resurrection of Jesus, the victory of God's kingdom of love and justice is on the way. Full and final victory is in the future, but the battle has begun and we know how it will end.

Thus, whenever we sing this hymn, God is already answering our petitions. God, the Almighty King, has already come to "reign over us," and will be "o'er all victorious." Jesus, the Incarnate Word, has already girt on his mighty sword and, in answer to our prayers, is making the proclamation of God's word successful. The comforting work of the Holy Spirit has already begun to "rule in every heart."

Of course, it doesn't appear to be actually happening that way in my neighborhood. It doesn't appear that God is King in our neighborhood arguments and affairs; it doesn't seem that God's word is inspiring the lives of all of my neighbors; God's rule by the Spirit in every heart isn't clearly evident.

Whether we pray for the coming of God's Kingdom in the words of the Lord's Prayer, or pray for the dawning of God's new day in the words of this hymn, there are scant signs in the real world that such an advent is on the way—at least, it doesn't look that way. But what if it is? What if, beneath surface appearances, God's work is secretly in progress?

If that is the case, if God is in loving pursuit of every one of my neighbors, that changes everything. It changes my entire attitude toward them. It makes me hopeful that, however far they may seem to be from the kingdom, God's grace is doing a lovingly subversive work in the depths of their hearts.

That, in turn, means that I must relate to them in reverence, seeking to affirm, in every possible way, God's secret work in their heart. I must be a friend to the most friendless, constantly "tuned to hear the slightest whisper" of the Spirit's presence. And I must be in that attitude of hopefulness toward the entire world beyond my neighborhood. Those of us who are followers of Jesus must become, as Sister Joan Chittister writes, "loving listeners to the heartbeat of the world."

But I wonder if my neighbors know that all of this is happening as they struggle to make ends meet and keep their lives and families together. Do they know what's really going on in our neighborhood?

It is my own guess that the little children do. I speak or wave to each of them as I pedal through the neighborhood each day. They know me by my first name and respond by saying "Hi" or else with a wave. One little girl from India has the most hopeful eyes I've ever seen, big, brown, and beautiful beyond description.

Have all children arrived in our world "trailing clouds of glory"? I don't mean that in Wordsworth's sense of having had a previous life elsewhere, but, instead, that it is written into our spiritual DNA as children that "all shall be well, and all manner of things shall be well."

However, like Eden's children, we are pushed out of this garden of innocence into a world in which the sweat of our brow washes this hopefulness away. Even so, are there moments when it all comes back and we know somehow that we've lost something along the way?

Sometimes I think I see a few of my neighbors struggling to recapture this lost memory. It's like when E. B. White would saunter along Third Avenue, looking into dim saloons where he'd see men leaning over the bar, "gazing steadily into the bottoms of glasses on the long chance that they could get another little peek at it"—at that lost sense of glory that God has built into the heart of every life.

What could be a more exciting purpose for my life than that of making my neighbors aware of this imprisoned splendor? By my prayers, actions, and words of hope and kindness, it is my mission to tell them that it is, indeed, "a beautiful day in this neighborhood," to invite them into this larger neighborhood of God, to say to them in the name of Jesus, "Please, won't you be my neighbor?"

Guide Me, O Thou Great Jehovah

1. Guide me, O thou great Je - ho - vah, pil - grim through this
2. O - pen now the cry - stal foun - tain, whence the heal - ing
3. When I tread the verge of Jor - dan, bid my anx - ious

bar - ren land. I am weak, but thou art migh - ty; hold me with thy
stream doth flow; let the fire and clou - dy pil - lar lead me all my
fears sub - side; death of death and hell's des - truc - tion, land me safe on

power - ful hand. Bread of hea - ven, bread of hea - ven, feed me
jour - ney through. Strong de - li - verer, strong de - li - verer, be thou
Ca - naan's side. Songs of prai - ses, songs of prai - ses, I will

till I want no more; (want no more) feed me till I want no more.
still my strength and shield; (stength and shield) be thou still my strength and shield.
e - ver give to thee; (give to thee) I will e - ver give to thee.

14

Guide Me, O Thou
Great Jehovah

This stirring hymn was written by the greatest Welsh hymn writer of the eighteenth century, William Williams. He was enormously popular in his own day and famous in history. He has been called as "the Isaac Watts of Wales" and the "Sweet Singer of Wales." One writer has concluded, "He did for Wales what Wesley and Watts did for England, or what Luther did for Germany."

Williams was born in 1717 and died in 1791. His birth place was Cefn-y-Coed in the parish of the famous Llanfair-y-bryn near Llandovery. He started out studying medicine but was converted by the famous and eloquent evangelical preacher, Howell Harris. He began studying for the ministry and was ordained as a deacon in the Church of England in 1740. Denied access to the priesthood, he quickly allied himself with the Calvinist Methodist movement in Wales.

For fifty years he served as an itinerant preacher throughout Wales, so it is not surprising that many of his hymns capture the idea of the pilgrimage of the Christian life. In his travels, he journeyed an average of about 3,000 miles per year for forty-five years. Often accompanied by his wife, who sang at his services, Williams wrote more than 800 hymns in Welsh and another one hundred in English. "Guide Me, O Thou Great Jehovah" has been fabulously popular and has been translated into more than seventy-five languages.

The first translation of the hymn was by Peter Williams, who was no relation, and published in 1771. The author

Williams accepted the translation but added another stanza and printed it as a leaflet entitled, "A Favorite Hymn sung by Lady Huntingdon's Young Collegians Printed by the desire of many Christians friends. Lord, give it thy blessing!" In the eighteenth century, titles weren't brief, but they did convey a lot of meaning, if not a great deal of feeling!

The tune, Cwm Rhondda, was composed by another Welshman, John Hughes, for a singing festival. It is named for the valley of the Rhondda River, a coal mining area in Wales.

The tune is a favorite at Welsh rugby matches, and it is common for the Welsh crowds to break out spontaneously during the course of a match and sing it to the players. It is so popular that it is considered the unofficial national anthem of Wales. Miners often sang it on the way to the mines. The story goes that this hymn was sung by Welsh soldiers in Flanders' Field during World War I, and the German soldiers were so moved by it that they joined in the singing.

"Guide Me, O Thou Great Jehovah" was also sung at Princess Diana's funeral and at the wedding of Prince William and Catherine Middleton. Those who remember the film *The African Queen* might recall that at the beginning of the film, Katherine Hepburn sings the hymn and plays the organ. When President James Garfield was assassinated and lay dying, his wife started singing this hymn to him. Garfield began to cry and said to Dr. Willard Bliss, his physician, "Glorious, Bliss, isn't it?"

John Hughes, the composer of this stirring tune of Cwm Rhondda, was born in Wales in 1873 and died there in 1932. He had virtually no formal education, and he worked in the coal and railroad industries. He was active in the Salem Baptist Church and followed his father as deacon and precentor (or song leader).

This hymn obviously evokes the theme of the Exodus and the experience of wandering in the wilderness ("pilgrim through this barren land"), yet it also incorporates references to manna in the wilderness and Christ ("Bread of heaven, feed me till I want no more"). The term, Jehovah, is the now unused name for God in the Old Testament, and some hymnbooks have altered this so that people sing, "Guide Me, O Thou Great Redeemer," which is the way the Mormon Tabernacle Choir sings it.

Williams subtitled the original version of this hymn, "A prayer of strength to go through the wilderness of the world." The experience of wandering in the wilderness is this hymn's most important spiritual insight—life as a pilgrimage, life as a road to be traveled. As the hymn explicitly states, this is not a journey we make alone. Rather, we are guided by God:

> I am weak but Thou art mighty;
> Hold me with Thy powerful hand.

And again:

> Strong deliverer, strong deliverer,
> Be Thou still my strength and shield.

One prominent biblical interpreter, Walter Brueggeman, has stated that the entire Bible can be summed up in one sentence: You are not alone.

That's what this hymn is all about.

Meditation

Songs of Praises

What is the first hymn that you remember from your childhood? What associations does it bring to your mind of Sunday school, church, or family?

Let me tell you about this hymn because it's the first one I remember and also because my earliest memories of it have no connection with any church or with any word in its verses. What I remember is the powerful tune, Cwn Rhondda, but I didn't know what was being sung because the words were in Welsh, that strange sounding Celtic language that I neither speak nor understand. Most of all, I remember how the men's voices would sweep upward on the final lines, "Pen Calfaria, Nac aed hwnw byth o'm cof."

I'm not even sure that those final lines translate into our English rendering as, "Songs of praises I will ever give to Thee." What I remember is the spiritual vigor with which they were sung.

The circumstance of these memories is that, although my family didn't attend church during my childhood, we did attend the monthly meetings of the local St. David's Society, one of many such associations at which folks of Welsh descent gather to celebrate and preserve their culture.

After a potluck dinner, the principal program of the evening was simply that of singing the great Welsh hymns, particularly this one. Singing hymns, as my colleague observes in the above introduction, is the principal pastime of the Welsh. However dangerous and difficult life may have been in the coal mines, Welshmen always found a way to keep singing. A Welsh neighbor of mine quotes a saying that declares, "Put a helmet on his head, give him a pick axe, and any Welshman will burst into song."

This national pastime has produced some grand men's choirs that join in large song festivals, such as one that was recorded in London's Royal Albert Hall, in which 5,000 men's voices could be heard singing this very hymn.

But now when I hear this hymn from my childhood, I think mostly of just one Welshman, my Uncle Will. The earliest photo I have of him was taken in 1881 in South Wales, in a photographer's studio in the city of Llanelly. It is a family photo of my grandmother and her first seven children, and was taken shortly before they came to America to join my grandfather, who had preceded them in the late 1870s.

Uncle Will, then nine years old, is standing in the second row, dressed elegantly in a suit and tie, even though the family was never prosperous. It was just the way things were done in those bygone days; you dressed in your best for a family photo.

I was never able to discover where, when, and how my Uncle Will got his religion, but he was the most devout member of that family that finally consisted of eleven children. Like his father, he worked in the iron mill until it passed out of existence with the advent of steel.

After that, he found whatever meager employment was available; in one job he served as his church's janitor. Even though he and Aunt Laura lived a threadbare life in a tiny house, their home was filled with songs of praises. They "said grace" before every meal and read a chapter of the Bible every night before going to bed.

I was in that happy home many times, but I was not there for the moment that I remember most, about which I was told by Aunt Laura. It came on that day in August 1945 when the news came over the radio that World War II had ended. We all knew that the announcement was coming and, in our homes and on the streets of our cities, were awaiting for the official word.

When it came, Uncle Will stood up reverently before the family radio and sang, "Praise God, from whom all blessings flow; Praise him, all creatures here below; Praise him above, ye heavenly host; Praise Father, Son, and Holy Ghost."

No voice teacher can teach you to sing like that, and you don't need to be Welsh to sing that way. Such grateful song is an entire way of life.

It arises from a life of simple faith in which we sing because God's Spirit is singing within us. It sings in the brightest day or in the darkest night. Such a life never stops singing, whatever befalls. When that deeper, simpler life of the Spirit takes over our lives, then we can truly sing, "Songs of praises, I will ever give to Thee."

Have you learned to live and to sing that way?

All Hail the Power of Jesus' Name

1 All hail the power of Jesus' name! Let an - gels
2 O seed of Is - rael's cho - sen race now ran - somed
3 Let ev - ery tongue and ev - ery tribe re - spon - sive
4 Oh, that with all the sa - cred throng we at his

pros - trate fall. Bring forth the roy - al di - a - dem,
from the fall, hail him who saves you by his grace,
to his call, to him all maj - es - ty as - cribe,
feet may fall! We'll join the ev - er - last - ing song.

Refrain

and crown him, crown him, crown him, crown him Lord of all!

15

All Hail the Power of Jesus' Name

This hymn is sometimes called "the National Anthem of Christendom" and has been translated into virtually every language spoken by Christians around the world. In the United States alone, it has been published in more than 2,300 hymnbooks.

The hymn is actually a composite creation of two authors, Edward Perronet and John Rippon. Perronet is credited with stanzas 1–3. Rippon altered stanzas two and three and wrote the fourth stanza.

Edward Perronet was born in 1726 and died in 1792. He was born into a family of French Huguenots (or French Calvinists) in Kent, England, and he was ordained as an Anglican priest. He had deep sympathies with the Wesleyan movement but broke with John Wesley over the administration of the sacraments, arguing that itinerant preachers should be able to celebrate communion. He ended his life as a Congregationalist minister.

His times were contentious and filled with controversy. Despite the ethereal quality of this hymn, one writer has said of Perronet, he was "a sharp-tongued, difficult personality, who would rather pick a fight over theology than display brotherly love."

The hymn was initially published anonymously with the title "On the Resurrection." As Perronet lay dying, his last words were: "Glory to God in the height of His divinity! Glory to God in the depth of His humanity! Glory to God in all His suffering! Into His Hands I commend my spirit."

His near contemporary was John R. Rippon, who was born in 1751 in Devonshire, England, and died in 1836 in London, where he had served as the pastor of a Baptist Church for an unbelievably long tenure of more than sixty years.

The tune, Coronation, was composed by Oliver Holden and published in a book of sacred music in 1793. The organ on which he wrote the tune is still on display in the Old State House in Boston. He lined out the tune just after the birth of his first daughter, and you might keep that in mind as you sing. After learning the origin of this hymn tune and at the birth of our granddaughter, Sarah, I found myself humming the music in my head!

Holden, a pioneer of American psalmody, was born in Shipley, Massachusetts, in 1765. He had minimal education and found work as a carpenter. He moved to Charlestown, Massachusetts when he was twenty-one and helped rebuild the town after it was burned by the British.

He became a prosperous realtor, founded singing schools, eventually became a representative to the Massachusetts legislature, and was active in the opposition to slavery. He organized music schools and compiled several collections of sacred music, and when General George Washington came to Boston in 1789, he helped organize the celebration and trained the choir.

There is an interesting irony in this hymn, written during and after the American Revolution. The War of Independence, as it is sometimes called, was a decisive break with the notion of kingship or royalty as a viable political idea and its replacement with the idea of democracy—a government of the people, by the people, and for the people.

And yet, this hymn takes the idea of royalty and attaches it to Jesus. You could say, as Christians have said throughout American history, that this is where the idea belongs and the only place it belongs. Yet, it's interesting that in ridding ourselves of kingship in the American Revolution, we American Christians have never wholly abandoned the idea of Christ as

King or the idea of the kingdom of God. Indeed, the theologian H. Richard Niebuhr wrote a book summarizing the entirety of American church history with the title, *The Kingdom of God in America.*

There are two conclusions that might be drawn. One is that the kingdom of God is never a kingdom of this world, and all pretensions of power should be measured by God's rule over all of human history. This idea has played an enormous role in social reform movements from the anti-slavery movement to the civil rights movement and the environmental movement.

Second, we as individuals should recognize God's reign in our own lives, even though we seek to control so much of our existence for our own benefit. That's a very hard lesson to learn, especially for many of us who have so much as a result of our own labors. As John Calvin put it, "We are not our own. We belong to God."

Or, as the hymn puts it,

O that with yonder sacred throng
We at his feet may fall!
We'll join the everlasting song,
And crown Him Lord of all!
We'll join the everlasting song,
And crown Him Lord of all!

If Christ is our King, then we are subject to Christ and should strive to follow him in all our ways.

Meditation

God's True Angels

"Let angels prostrate fall." How interesting that so many of our hymns mention angels, despite the fact that persons of good faith in many religions have such different and even opposing views about the existence and activity of angels.

In recent years there has been a resurgence of interest in angels. While browsing through a popular shopping mall bookstore at the height of this revival of angelology, I discovered that there were more books about angels than about Jesus. Even though that wave of interest has receded, there are devout persons still who report receiving guidance and support from such celestial visitations.

Many other persons of similar good faith and practice have their doubts. They will sing hymns and carols that make mention of angels; however, if pressed for an explanation of their actual belief, they will say that angels represent the ancient mythological manner in which people of a pre-scientific age expressed their experience of God's mysterious, providential care.

So, they would say, "We continue to sing about angels, but know in our minds that God doesn't really need their help in the management of our world." Those who study their Bibles carefully will even call attention to Isaiah's utterly monotheistic statement, "I am the Lord, and there is no other, besides me there is no God; I equip you, though you do not know me, . . . I am the Lord, who does all these things" (Isa 45:5, 7).

There you have it, right in Scripture. God is all there is and doesn't need a heavenly court of angelic helpers to know what's what and do what needs doing. Which is to say that St. Benedict was a bit over the top when he said that God knows about our actions because of the fact that they are "reported by angels at every hour."

We will not resolve our differing viewpoints about angelic activity on this page. A reverent agnosticism may befit both believers and skeptics. We can neither prove not disprove the existence of angels, any more than we can prove or disprove the existence of God. All this stuff about angels in the Bible may be reminding us that there is more to our universe than we can see, and that unseen influences for good may surround us and shape our lives in ways we will never be able to explain.

But there's a better way to be thinking about angels because we're all supposed to be "good angels," by which I mean good messengers, the literal meaning of "evangelists." Many people are unaware that the word "angel" is one of the roots of the word evangelist (*eu=good, aggelos=messenger*).

This doesn't mean that we become the kind of people who go about asking strangers if they're saved. Nor does it mean that we become those obsessive do-gooders, the kind of people who have such a "need to be needed" that the needy whom they pursue can be identified by the hunted expression on their faces. Being truly good angels can be something entirely and quietly quite different.

A Sufi story tells about a man who was so good that angels were sent to him with the offer that he be granted three things: the gift to heal the sick, the power to convert others, and the beauty of a virtuous life. When the man, in humility, declined all three, the angels insisted that he choose one. So he asked that he might be able to do great good in the world without ever knowing about it.

The angels then devised the following answer to his request: wherever his shadow fell *behind* him, people would be cured, the grieving would be comforted, the weak would be strengthened, children would grow, and crops would flourish. Wherever he went in the world, everyone and everything would be somehow better because of his shadow, but he would never know what had happened because it occurred behind his back.

Eventually, all that people remembered was that his shadow was healing. And after a long time, even his name was forgotten; people spoke of him only as "the Holy Shadow."

The really good and great angels who visit our world have no name. They have no knowledge of all the good they have done, and seek no final recognition for their healing work. They leave behind no monuments, buildings, or endowments to perpetuate the memory of their goodness. They do not harbor the secret dream that hundreds of mourners will attend their funeral, and that wonderful eulogies will tell of all the good they have done.

They do not even envision a heavenly awards banquet at which, before all the hosts of heaven, their good works will, at last, be recognized. Their favorite Bible verse is John 3:30, in which John the Baptist says of Jesus, "He must increase, but I must decrease." They live with the delicious secret that God alone knows what good they have done and has met them with the words, "Well done, good and faithful servant."

These are the real angels; we seldom, if ever, know their names, but what we experience is their healing shadow.

Glorious Things of Thee Are Spoken

1 Glo - rious things of thee are spo - ken, Zi - on, ci - ty of our God;
2 See the streams of li - ving wa - ters, spring - ing from e - ter - nal love,
3 Round each ha - bi - ta - tion ho - vering, see the cloud and fire ap - pear,
4 Sa - vior, since of Zi - on's ci - ty I through grace a mem - ber am,

he whose Word can - not be bro - ken formed you for his own a - bode.
well sup - ply your sons and daugh - ters and all fear of want re - move.
for a glo - ry and a cov - ering, sho - wing that the Lord is near!
let the world de - ride or pi - ty, I will glo - ry in your name.

On the Rock of A - ges foun - ded, what can shake your sure re - pose?
Who can faint while such a ri - ver e - ver flows their thirst as- suage?
Thus de - ri - ving from their ban - ner light by night and shade by day,
Fa - ding are the world's best plea - sures, all its bloat - ed pomp and show;

With sal - va - tion's walls sur - roun - ded, you may smile at all your foes.
Grace, which like the Lord, the gi - ver, ne - ver fails from age to age.
safe they feed up - on the man - na which God gives them on their way.
so - lid joys and las - ting trea - sure none but Zi - on's chil - dren know.

16

Glorious Things
of Thee Are Spoken

We now turn to two hymns by the great hymn writer and Christian visionary, John Newton—"Glorious Things of Thee Are Spoken" and "Amazing Grace."

Newton is well known to many people because of the beautiful movie, *Amazing Grace*, and the moving documentary by Bill Moyers of the same name. Here is an outline of his life that has resulted in these two hymns of remarkable beauty.

The story is filled with sheer drama. Newton was born in 1725. His mother died when he was seven. His father was an English sea captain, and Newton went to sea at age eleven. He went on many voyages through the Mediterranean and to the West Indies and eventually became a slave-ship captain at the height of the slave trade.

His conversion was influenced by reading Thomas á Kempis's *Imitation of Christ*, the guidance of a fellow ship captain, and the terror of being caught in a tumultuous storm at sea. He studied for the ministry, sought ordination, and served as a minister with distinction.

During these years he wrote poems and hymns, and died at age eighty-three, full of grace and highly respected everywhere. He preached until almost the end of his life, asking, "Shall the old African blasphemer stop while he can speak?"

On his long and lonely sea voyages, Newton educated himself by mastering Euclidian mathematics, learning Latin to read Virgil and Erasmus, studying the Bible (in Hebrew and Greek), and conducting Sunday worship for his crews.

A friend of the Wesleys and the revivalist George White-field, he applied for ordination in the Church of England but was refused. Eventually, in 1764, he was appointed to the evangelical curacy of the church at Olney, composed almost entirely of poor people, and then accepted appointment to a church in London.

At Olney, Newton soon became known as a powerful preacher, and his little church needed to add a gallery to accommodate the crowds that came to hear him. The poet William Cowper moved to Olney and collaborated with Newton in publishing the famous "Olney Hymns." Newton himself contributed nearly 300 hymns, including "Glorious Things of Thee Are Spoken" and "Amazing Grace." Newton often wrote hymns to complement his sermons, sometimes one each week.

He could never forget the anguish of his former slave-trade experiences, and in later years, Newton became the inspiring influence on William Wilberforce, who led the fight against slavery in Britain. Newton held on to life just long enough to witness Parliament's abolition of slavery in 1807.

As a sign of his impact on both sides of the Atlantic, Newton received an honorary degree in 1792 from what is now Princeton University. Two other recipients of honorary degrees at the same ceremony were Alexander Hamilton and Thomas Jefferson.

Before he died, he prepared his own epitaph that read, in part:

> John Newton, once an infidel and libertine, a servant of slaves in Africa, was, by the rich mercy of our Lord and Saviour, Jesus Christ, preserved, restored, pardoned, and appointed to preach the faith he had long laboured to destroy.

The tune to "Glorious Things of Thee Are Spoken" is "Austria," a stirring composition by Franz Joseph Haydn. It was composed in 1797 as a "Volkslied" or "folk song" by Haydn, who was serving as the Chapel Master to the Austrian Emperor Franz Josef. It was dedicated to the Emperor and first performed on the Emperor's birthday, February 12, 1797.

It set to music a patriotic prayer by Lorenz Leopold Haschka, modeled on "God Save the King." This was the era of the French Revolution, the rise of Napoleon, and growing nationalism. England had its national hymn; France adopted the "Marseillaise" as its anthem in 1795. Haydn gave Austria its counterpart in 1797.

It met with instant success. Haydn wrote it initially for piano and then expanded it for accompaniment by a small orchestra. Haydn later incorporated it into one of his most famous quartets, "The Emperor." Eric Routley declared that it "stands as one of the very few examples of a first-class hymn-tune written by a symphonic composer of the front rank."

Germany adopted the tune for its national anthem, and by 1802 it was already picked up by British and American hymn writers. It appeared in a German hymnbook in 1804, so within five years this inspiring masterpiece was widely sung across Europe and North America.

Please pay attention to the second stanza of the hymn and remember that Newton was writing for his impoverished congregation at Olney:

See, the streams of living waters,
Springing from eternal love,
Well supply thy sons and daughters,
And all fear of want remove.
Who can faint while such a river
Ever flows their thirst to assuage?
Grace, which like the Lord the giver,
Never fails from age to age.

In the midst of dire poverty, in the midst of deprivation, this is a hymn that gives a simple message: God provides.

And in the midst of our own anxiety and anguish and suffering, John Newton reminds us: Fear not. God provides.

———————

Meditation

A Sweet Little Nest—In the City?

Of all the hymns we are considering, those who want to sing this hymn with understanding will need to do quite a bit of Bible reading in order to sort out its mixed Scriptural references.

The opening words are taken from Psalm 87, a song of praise about the biblical city of Jerusalem, but one that is somewhat obscure in its ancient references. From there, the hymn takes us to scenes of the wilderness journey in Exodus, as we read how God's people were protected by the pillar of cloud by day and the pillar of fire by night, and fed miraculously by a daily supply of manna.

From there, as we sing of the river that "ever flows their thirst to assuage," we are sent to the New Testament, and to the last pages of our Bible where (Rev 21, 22) we see that other city, the New Jerusalem, through which flows the river of the water of life.

Newton's mind, unlike ours today, seems to have been so drenched with Scripture that he moved easily from one biblical metaphor to another. It is not always easy to keep up with him. However, despite its mixed metaphors, this hymn helps us see one thing clearly. Our life's journey as the children of God is moving in the direction of a city.

It has always been that way. Since Abraham, who "looked forward to the city that has foundations, whose architect and builder is God," God's people have been moving toward an ideal city. Ancient Jerusalem didn't become that perfect city, but even after its destruction by the armies of Babylon, God's word through Jeremiah to the captives who had been carried away to Babylon was, "But seek the welfare of the city where I have sent you into exile, and pray to the LORD on its behalf, for in its welfare you will find your welfare."

Then, centuries later, after the first Jerusalem had been rebuilt and destroyed again by the armies of Rome, John's apocalyptic vision is still of a city, the Holy City, the New Jerusalem, coming down from God out of heaven. Interesting also is the fact that although the Bible begins in a country garden, it ends in a city.

We've always been moving away from that garden, looking eastward from Eden, moving toward the sunrise of a new day in an ideal city. Indeed, in classic Christian architecture, we've built our churches so that our altars faced eastward! In one of our Advent hymns we even sing, "People, look east!" Our true life has always awaited us eastward from Eden in the city. But that has not been the tribal dream of our culture. Listen to this one:

> With someone like you, a pal good and true,
> I'd like to leave it all behind and go and find
> A place that's known to God alone,
> Just a spot to call our own.
>
> We'll find perfect peace where joys never cease,
> Somewhere beneath the starry skies.
> We'll build a sweet little nest somewhere in the west,
> And let the rest of the world go by.

That 1919 ballad that just won't go away. Recorded by the wildest, widest array of singers, it has been sung since the Roaring Twenties, through the Great Depression, then the war years, on the silver screen, or in country music venues. Everyone wants to sing it. Why?

Because it appeals to both old and young audiences, and expresses our dream to somehow "get away from it all." Even if you've never heard this ballad, it tells the story of our times, as we've been moving out of the cities to find seclusion in the suburbs, our stores and churches making their exodus with us. Some with greater resources have moved even beyond the suburbs to the countryside.

But however we design our perfect getaway (and for some it could be a simple cottage by a pond), what happens to those who find their heavenly nest in the west? The Bible and the saints warn us to beware.

When we no longer need people, when we finally get away from the madding crowd and have it all our way, we won't be in heaven, but in the deepest hell. Hell is where we don't have to think about anyone other than our self. Hell is where I experience Frank Sinatra's ultimate isolation of doing it "my way."

If we ever find that perfect nest in the west, if we ever get to the point at which we have no need of other people, we're on our way downward into the deepest hell.

Barbra Streisand had it at least half-right when she sang, "People who need people are the luckiest people in the world." People who need people are not only the luckiest people, they're the people of God.

Even if people are not religious in the traditional sense, if they have figured out that there's no real life without people, they're not far from the kingdom of God. Ask anyone making progress in a recovery program, and they'll tell you how true it is that when we realize that we need people, we're moving in a heavenly direction.

So what does this say about our life today? Whether we live in some lovely country home, or in some high-rise apartment "where cross the crowded ways of life," it tells us that God's goal for human life is that we live together in community, and that we can start becoming citizens of that heavenly Zion today.

To do so, we'll have to start practicing those rules for kingdom living, about which we've been praying all of our lives. The basic rules provide food and forgiveness for everyone. In the

New Jerusalem, we ask only for our daily bread. It's just as it was on that long-ago wilderness journey; we get our manna one day at a time. Try to hoard more for tomorrow, and it goes rotten (Exod 16:21).

In God's city, everyone has enough because no one tries to have more than enough of the necessities of life. In the same way, there's forgiveness for everyone, because we learn that we can know the freedom of forgiveness only as we forgive everyone else.

And the very best thing about the Holy City is that its gates will never be shut (Rev 21:25). Even for those who have hoarded themselves into the deepest hell, the gates will always be open; there'll always be a room for them, always be vacancies in the New Jerusalem!

We can start living as citizens of that glorious city today. We can make our lives and our neighborhoods tiny samples of the Holy City. God can open us up and make us open people with open minds and open hearts, the kind of people who sojourn through life singing, "we're marching upward to Zion, the beautiful city of God."

Amazing Grace—How Sweet the Sound

1 A - maz - ing grace— how sweet the sound—
2 'Twas grace that taught my heart to fear,
3 The Lord has prom - ised good to me,
4 Through man - y dan - gers, toils, and snares
5 When we've been there ten thou - sand years,

that saved a wretch like me! I once was lost
and grace my fears re - lieved; how pre - cious did
his word my hope se - cures; he will my shield
I have al - read - y come; 'tis grace hath brought
bright shin - ing as the sun, we've no less days

but now am found, was blind but now I see.
that grace ap - pear the hour - I first be - lieved!
and por - tion be as long as life en - dures.
me safe thus far, and grace will lead me home.
to sing God's praise than when we'd first be - gun.

17

Amazing Grace—
How Sweet the Sound

This is undoubtedly the best known and the most loved of all the hymns. One of John Newton's biographers estimates that it is performed aboutl ten million times annually.

"Amazing Grace" does not appear in Robert Coote's "hymn hit parade" that we are using for this book. The main reason is that "Amazing Grace" never made it into English hymnals until the twentieth century. In fact, the first time it appeared was in 1964. The nineteenth-century hymnologist John Julian explained its omission by snootily saying that it was "far from being a good example of Newton's work."

On this side of the Atlantic, however, the fate of "Amazing Grace" was very different. It has always been a stunning success.

Newton's *Olney Hymns* probably came over to the United States with the Scotch Presbyterians, who settled in Kentucky and Tennessee. It was especially popular at Methodist camp meetings, and in 1835 it appeared in the hymnbook, *Southern Harmony*, with the now standard New Britain tune. *Southern Harmony* took the scene by storm, especially in the South. Approximately 600,000 copies were sold, representing about one copy for every forty people in the U.S. at that time. However, "Amazing Grace" didn't appear in many of the northern hymnals.

Part of the reason for this curious reception may lie in the fact that, in the original version of "Amazing Grace," there is no mention of God in the first three stanzas. The fourth stanza was added later by Newton, and the fifth stanza comes from a hymnbook published in 1790. So it may be that theological purity played a role in shunting this gorgeous hymn temporarily to the sidelines.

Another is the hymn's principal virtue—simplicity. "Amazing Grace" is "simply" beautiful. It contains none of the complexity and ostentation of the hymnody of the eighteenth and nineteenth centuries. It was written for poor people, and Newton wrote it to follow his sermon and emphasize the point. In its original version, it had only eleven words with more than one syllable.

But if Newton wrote it for poor people, it's clearly a hymn for everyone, and in the twentieth century, it became the most widely performed song there is. It has moved out of the South to become a mainstream tune for both sacred and secular audiences.

Mahalia Jackson performed it on the radio in 1947 and included it in one of her albums. Judy Collins sung it as an anti-Vietnam war protest song during the sixties. Others who have recorded it include Aretha Franklin, Johnny Cash, Elvis Presley, and Willie Nelson. Arlo Guthrie sang it in 1969 at Woodstock. It's been featured in movies, such as *Alice's Restaurant, Coal Miner's Daughter*, and *Silkwood*. It was sung after the 1995 Oklahoma City bombing and after 9/11. The Library of Congress has recordings of "Amazing Grace" by more than 450 artists.

The tune, "New Britain," first appeared in a hymnbook published in 1831, known as *Virginia Harmony*. We don't know the origin of the tune, but it may have been an African melody. Because of Newton's early life as a slave-ship captain, that makes "Amazing Grace" all the more powerful and poignant.

Two final points about Newton's famous hymn. First, at the beginning we sing:

> Amazing grace, how sweet the sound,
> That saved a wretch like me.

Some people recoil at the use of "wretch," but it's based on Newton's own life. During Newton's years as a sailor, he once ran afoul of the captain, who demoted him to the lowest rank of seamen on the ship. This rank was known as "a wretch."

So Newton isn't using a theological term in this hymn but a seafaring term with theological implications.

Second, this hymn also recalls the Apostle Paul's conversion when scales fell from his eyes:

> I once was lost, but now I'm found,
> Was blind, but now I see.

Who among us can sing those words and *not* recall a time when we were lost and then found, when we were blind and then could see?

Or who can sing those words and not pray, "God, open my eyes. God, make me see"?

Meditation

Pursued by Kindness

When I became a genuine, born-again, true believer in my late teens, "Amazing Grace" was high on the hymn hit parade in the church I had begun to attend. In fact, it was so high on my list that the first tutorial paper I prepared for my graduate preceptor during my freshman year at a very secular college was about its author, John Newton.

Back in the 1940s, "Amazing Grace" had not begun to be the popular song that it has become in our day, as country music stars and other recording celebrities include it in their albums of otherwise worldly pop favorites.

I confess, however, that one of my motives for writing the paper was to bear witness to my newfound faith to my preceptor with whom I would have a one-on-one relationship throughout my freshman year. The story of Newton's conversion and the gradual ending of his old life as captain of a slave ship, I thought, might even result in the conversion of my preceptor.

My preceptor had heard neither of the hymn nor of Newton and gave me a good mark for a decent piece of historical research but, apparently, was never saved as the result of my subtle evangelistic effort. Even so, my preceptor was a decent, friendly graduate student who, even after our tutorial year had ended, continued to show genuine interest in me in the years that followed.

I feel embarrassed as I think back upon the hubris with which I, as a lowly freshman, had presumed to make myself the spiritual guide of an instructor whose academic level far exceeded mine and whose life experience as a battle veteran of World War II may have formed him spiritually far beyond my own limited boundaries.

How gracious that he accepted me "just as I was." It would take me many years to realize the unrecognized spiritual pride of my early post-conversion days and, even more, the radically amazing depth of God's grace.

I would have to travel down many wrong roads and dead end streets to become sufficiently sadder and wiser so as to understand the stark statement in the Letter to the Ephesians (2:8, 9), "For by grace you have been saved through faith, and *this is not your own doing; it is the gift of God.*"

I thought that I had something to do with my experience of rebirth; at the very least, I had accepted God's offer of salvation. But here it was in black and white on the pages of my New Testament: this was not my own doing!

It had somehow escaped my attention that my very ability to believe was a gift, that it was God who had awakened the gift of faith within me. How could I have missed the plain fact that, just as I made no decision about being born in 1928, neither did I make a decision to be reborn in 1945? Those great moments of decision were made for me, the first by my father and mother, the second by our heavenly Father.

It took me many years to realize that grace is truly amazing, amazing in the sense that becoming a Christian was not my own doing, but simply and solely a gift of God.

However, as I began to realize the "amazingness" of grace, I began to recall steps along the way in which a mysterious presence seemed to be pursuing my life, preparing me for "the hour I first believed." And then, much later when I was studying Hebrew, I discovered a wonderful verse in the all time hit parade of Psalms.

Nearly all of us have memorized those final words in Psalm 23:6, "Surely goodness and mercy shall follow me all the days of my life." However, if we translate the Hebrew words literally, that verse sounds even more amazing: "Only goodness and grace (*hesed*, the Hebrew term for God's grace and kindness) shall *pursue* me all the days of my life."

That's what has been happening through all the days of our lives. Since the day of our birth, although we are unaware of it, God's grace has been pursuing us. Being "saved by grace" is not a one-time event; it is happening all through our lives as God surrounds us with all kinds of events by which grace will lead us home.

A chance meeting with some saint who, uninvited, suddenly shows up and speaks the one word that we needed to hear; a career disappointment that sends us down another road that becomes God's appointment of a better plan for our lives; a complete crash that brings us so far down that, for the first time, we can look up and live—all of these accidents of grace do for us what we could never have hoped, planned, or done for ourselves.

And now, many years later, I even wonder if I experienced grace from that "unsaved" preceptor of my freshman year. His acceptance of me "just as I am" was, really, what grace is all about, what God is doing for us on every day of our lives, loving us as we are today so that, we can finally become, in Christ, all that we're meant to be tomorrow.

As a friend has written, grace is "that acceptance which is greater than all our dysfunction, that long embrace out of which we cannot squirm." Yes, indeed, it is not our own doing. It is unmerited, unexpected, uninvited, and unconditional. Now that's amazing!

Some unknown poet was so moved by the amazing depth of God's grace that he or she did not even attach their name to these verses:

> I sought the Lord, and afterward I knew
> He moved my soul to seek him, seeking me;
> It was not I that found, O Saviour true;
> No, I was found of Thee.

> I find, I walk, I love, but O the whole
> Of love is but my answer, Lord, to Thee!
> For Thou wert long beforehand with my soul;
> Always Thou lovedst me.

How Firm a Foundation

1 How___ firm a foun - da - tion, you saints of the Lord,
2 "Fear___ not, I am with you, O be not dis - mayed,
3 "When___ through the deep wa - ters I call you to go,
4 "When___ through fie - ry tri - als your path - way shall lie,
5 "The___ soul that on Je - sus still leans for re - pose,

is___ laid for your faith in his ex - cel - lent Word!
for___ I am your God and will still give you aid;
the___ ri - vers of sor - row shall not o - ver - flow;
my___ grace, all suf - fi - cient shall be your sup - ply;
I___ will not, I will not de - sert to its foes;

What more can he say than to you he has said,
I'll streng - then you, help you, and cause you to stand,
for I will be with you, your trou - bles to bless,
the flame shall not hurt you, I on - ly de - sign
that soul, though all hell should en - dea - vor to shake,

to you who for re - fuge to Je - sus have fled?
u - pheld by my right - eous, o - mni - po - tent hand.
and___ sanc - ti - fy to you your deep - est dis - tress.
your dross to con - sume, and your gold to re - fine.
I'll ne - ver, no ne - ver, no ne - ver for - sake!"

18

How Firm a Foundation

This hymn originally appeared in John Rippon's *A Selection of Hymns*, published in 1787. Rippon was an English Baptist minister, and this hymnbook made him famous and wealthy because it contained a selection of hymns by Isaac Watts and by what he called "the best authors." Later editions attribute the authorship of the hymn to Kn or K or Keen.

What seems fairly certain is that the author of the hymn is Richard Keen, the precentor or song leader in the London church where John Rippon was pastor. Hymnologists have been frustrated by Rippon because he frequently did not credit the authors of hymns and altered their texts without indicating the changes.

It wouldn't be the last time that church musicians didn't get enough credit.

Rippon's hymnbook was a great success on both sides of the Atlantic, except in the Church of England, which has never printed this hymn in any of its hymnbooks. However, it has been a staple in Episcopal hymnals in the United States.

"How Firm a Foundation" was sung at the funerals of Robert E. Lee, Woodrow Wilson, and Theodore Roosevelt. It was a favorite of Andrew Jackson's wife, and when Andrew Jackson was dying, he asked that it be sung to him.

The tune, "Foundation," is an American folk melody originally called "Protection." This practice of matching hymn texts to folk music was quite common in the United States, especially among evangelicals. It reminds one of what Luther did during the Reformation—using tavern tunes for singing hymns.

"Foundation" first appeared in a hymnbook entitled, *Genuine Church Music*, edited by Joseph Funk and published in 1832. Funk was a jack of all trades—farmer, singing-school teacher, and music publisher.

Interestingly, Funk's hymnbook remains in print and is still used by Mennonites in the Shenandoah Valley.

The text uses 2 Corinthians and Hebrews (the last verse of the hymn), but the hymn text is primarily based on Isaiah 43:2–5, but also Isaiah 41:10, which reads:

> Do not fear, for I am with you
>> Do not be afraid, for I am your God.
> I will strengthen you, I will help you
>> I will uphold you with my victorious right hand.

This is obviously a hymn of faith and trust sung to our God, who is faithful to us and trustworthy. It's a sturdy hymn, to be sung with gusto and feeling.

Let me illustrate this with an autobiographical illustration. Just after the reunion of the Presbyterian Church in 1983, I had the honor to serve as the chair of a special committee charged with designing the new seal of the Church. I first declined saying I had no training in art, but the moderator, Sarah Bernice Moseley, insisted that the committee needed someone who knew the history of the church. Somewhat grudgingly, I agreed to do it.

I never had so much fun in all my life. We ended up with a splendid symbol, created by the famous graphic designer Malcolm Grear, but then we had to get it approved by the General Assembly. Grear was astonished and very anxious that his art had to be voted on by 700 people.

I worked with a very creative media expert on the General Assembly staff, Bill Gee, and together we produced an audio-visual presentation for the Assembly. It showed the component parts of the seal—dove, fire, cross, cup, etc., and then brought it all together at the end.

During the first part of the presentation, "How Firm a Foundation" was played in the background to suggest the sturdiness of the Reformed faith and the firm structure of the symbol. In the second part, we played "Amazing Grace."

I wanted "How Firm a Foundation" because that's what the seal represents and that's what our faith in God is when we rely upon God's love. I wanted "Amazing Grace" as the conclusion because it captures so well the stunning and surprising forgiveness of God. I was also convinced that people would respond favorably if you played "Amazing Grace" to them.

It worked. After the audio visual presentation, the Assembly gave Malcolm Grear a standing ovation, and the next day the Assembly approved the seal unanimously.

So, as you sing "How Firm a Foundation," think about the order and structure of the Christian faith, the reliability and faithfulness of God, but most of all think about this:

> When through the deep waters I call thee to go,
> The rivers of sorrow shall not overflow;
> For I will be near thee, thy troubles to bless,
> And sanctify to thee thy deepest distress.

And,

> The soul that on Jesus hath leaned for repose,
> I will not, I will not desert to its foes;
> That soul, though all hell should endeavor to shake,
> I'll never, no, never, no, never forsake.

Meditation

Never, No Never, No Never!

Don't ever omit that fifth verse of this hymn. Sometimes it's printed at the bottom of the page, but don't you ever skip it!

The soul that on Jesus hath leaned for repose,
I will not, I will not desert to his foes;
That soul, though all hell should endeavor to shake,
I'll never, no never, no never forsake.

My twin sons had "leaned for repose" upon one another in their mother's womb during the months before they were born prematurely and, after that traumatic entrance into our world, were not about to be separated. In the first few weeks after their arrival, they were most content being in the same crib.

After that, of course, they accepted being placed in their own cribs, but only if the cribs were placed next to one another so that they could reach through the bars of their "cages" and be in physical touch with one another.

I'm not sure how an early childhood specialist would regard this arrangement, but it made it possible to get more sleep if they were content with this procedure. As they grew stronger, however, they learned to climb over the railing of the crib and be back where they started, in the same crib.

This, of course, was dangerous; they could easily fall as they climbed over into the next crib. So, long before the usual time for such a change, it was time to put them in separate beds—twin beds, of course. We made much of this new plan, telling them of how they were now big boys with their very own "big boy beds."

To make the change even more appealing, we placed the twin beds flush against one another. They could now be in their own bed but still reach over and be in touch. Problem solved!

Well—not quite. After rehearsing with them how wonderful their new night life would be, we said their prayers and settled down for a good night's rest.

Before finally retiring ourselves, we went in to check on them. The plan had worked, but in their favor. They were fast asleep, entwined with one another, but in one bed. The problem with being identical, being fully identified with another person, is that we become inseparable.

One of the earliest Christian hymns (Phil 2:7) states that Christ Jesus was "born in human likeness." Jesus identified himself with us in our humanity, became identical with us. Indeed, "Having become human, he stayed human" (as translated in *The Message*).

This was not a temporary masquerade. The humanity of Jesus was not a costume, like the street clothes of the mild-mannered reporter, Clark Kent, under which human trappings, he was always Superman. To believe that about the humanity of Jesus is to fall into that early heresy, Gnosticism, whose adherents believed that Jesus was never truly human; it was all a masquerade.

But our Scriptures and creeds have insisted that this was not such a temporary costume; instead, Jesus became one of us. And my belief is that it was not simply a generic identification, an identification with humanity in general. God's incarnation in my life is so radically individual that George MacDonald prays, "Come thou, holy Love, . . . possess me utterly, for thou art more me than I am myself."

In a previous meditation, I recalled how our lives are a story of mysterious "if" factors, the big one being that if my father and mother had not met and married, I would never have been born. They could have married other partners; there could have been other children, but there would never have been that unique blending of their two lives that resulted in the birth of the "one and only" me!

I am the only special me in all the universe. From my parent's marriage, there might have been a brother or sister born before or after me (there were none), but I'm the only me there is or ever has been! And that says something radically wonderful about the incarnation of Jesus Christ in our humanity: Jesus became uniquely human in each one of us. He became human just as Morgan Roberts is human.

There is some facet of God's glory in Jesus Christ that can be reflected only in my life. My life has something particularly glorious to reveal about Jesus that can be expressed only through my life. To make Jesus known to the world in that special way is the highest purpose of my existence.

For this I was born, and if it doesn't happen in and through my life, it can't happen in that unique way in any other life. Other lives can reflect their own unique gleam of Jesus' glory, but not in the same way in which it can shine through my life. Jesus died and rose again not just for all humankind, but in particular for me, and I don't believe that he will ever give up on me until God's eternal purpose for my life is fully and finally realized.

He'll never, no never, no never give up on me. He has made himself so identical with me that we are inseparable. In the darkest night he entwines himself with me. I'll never have to sleep alone!

And all of this is true of your life. There's something to be said about Jesus that can be said only by John Mulder, or by you, and you, and you, whatever your name, whatever your story, whatever your sins, and whatever your failures. Jesus will never be satisfied until you are all that God has meant you to be from all eternity. Nothing will ever be able to separate you from God's design for your life in Jesus Christ.

And this is true whether you've made a worldly success of your life or if you're a seemingly helpless, hopeless failure, finding bed and board in a soup kitchen. It's never, no never, no never with you and Jesus.

So, it has to be the same between you and me too. If you're that precious to God, that inseparable from Jesus, then I must never give up on you, whoever you are. If I want to follow Jesus, then I'll have to find some way to say those same, wonderful words to you: because of Jesus' inseparable identification with you, I'll never, no never, no never forsake you! I may not be the best mate in all the world, but you're stuck with me, just as Jesus is stuck with me, and also with you . . . forever!

Holy, Holy, Holy,
Lord God Almighty

1 Ho - ly, ho - ly, ho - ly! Lord__ God Al - migh - ty!
2 Ho - ly, ho - ly, ho - ly! All the saints a - dore thee,
3 Ho - ly, ho - ly, ho - ly! though the dark - ness hide thee,
4 Ho - ly, ho - ly, ho - ly! Lord__ God Al - migh - ty!

Ear - ly in the mor - ning our song shall rise to thee.
cas - ting down their gol - den crowns a - round the glas - sy sea;
though the eye made blind by sin thy glo - ry may not see,
All thy works shall praise thy name, in earth, and sky, and sea;

Ho - ly, ho - ly, ho - ly! Mer - ci - ful and migh - ty!
che - ru - bim and se - ra - phim fal - ling down be - fore thee,
on - ly thou art ho - ly; there is none be - side thee,
Ho - ly, ho - ly, ho - ly! Mer - ci - ful and migh - ty!

God in three Per - sons, bles - sèd Tri - ni - ty!
which wert and art, and e - ver - more shalt be.
per - fect in power, in love and pu - ri - ty.
God in three per - sons, bles - sèd Tri - ni - ty!

19

Holy, Holy, Holy, Lord God Almighty

This is the most popular of the hymns by the influential Reginald Heber, who lived a highly creative but all too brief life. He was born in Malpas, England in 1783 and educated at Oxford, where he won prizes for his poetry. He was ordained in 1807 and became vicar of his family's estate in Shropshire. During this time he wrote hymns because he tired of the poor singing by his congregation and because he wanted the Church of England to have more good songs like the Methodists and Baptists.

All told, Heber wrote fifty-seven hymns, which are marked by beauty and awe. Heavily influenced by the Romantic movement, he is considered the father of Romantic hymnody, and one historian credits him with writing "the purest poetry in English hymnody. . . . The age of true hymnody in the Church of England had its beginnings with him."

Heber longed to be a missionary, and in 1823 he was appointed Bishop of Calcutta. He threw himself into the work, traveling and preaching ceaselessly. He ordained the first native Indian Christian in India. After three years of constant work, he died suddenly in 1826. On the day of his death, he baptized forty-two people and preached in torrid heat to a large crowd. Afterwards he dove into a cool pool and suffered a fatal stroke. He was only forty-three.

His wife collected his hymns and published them as *Hymns Written and Adapted to the Weekly Church Services of the Year* in 1827, the first hymnbook arranged according to the church year.

The hymn of praise to the Trinity is based on prophetic and apocalyptic passages in Isaiah 6 and Revelation 4:8–11 and Revelation 5 and 15. It is included in virtually every hymnal in the English language. Alfred Lord Tennyson called it the greatest hymn in the English language.

One hymn by Heber has achieved lasting controversy and notoriety. It's a missionary hymn called "From Greenland's Icy Mountains." It appalled Gandhi and became a lightning rod for Hindus and adherents of other faiths who complained about Christian "aggression" toward their beliefs.

The line that infuriated Gandhi was "where every prospect pleases, and man alone is vile." Gandhi declared, "You, the missionaries, come to India thinking that you come to a land of heathens, of idolaters, of men who do not know God. . . . I wish [Bishop Heber] had not written [those lines]. My own experience in my travels throughout India has been to the contrary. I have gone from one end of the country to the other, without any prejudice, in a relentless search after truth, and I am not able to say that here in this fair land . . . man is vile. He is as much a seeker after truth as you and I are, possibly more so."

Defenders of Heber argue that what he meant was the sinfulness of all humanity, not those alone in the Indian subcontinent. Nevertheless, Gandhi's complaint had great truth in it, and fortunately the missionary movement has learned from it and now demonstrates much more respect for other cultures and other religions.

The tune, "Nicea," was composed by John Bacchus Dykes, and it is called Nicea because the text illuminates the doctrine of the Trinity developed in the Council of Nicea and embodied in the Nicene Creed, one of the most important Christian confessions. One historian has maintained that the tune Nicea "has given [the hymn] a matchless glory all over the world." Another has written that "on the strength of [Nicea] alone Dykes earns immortality in the annals of hymnody."

Dykes was one of the finest nineteenth-century English composers of church music and an Anglican priest. He was born in Hull, England, and from an early age he could play by ear. At the age of ten he was the assistant organist in his grandfather's church. He studied at Cambridge and was cofounder of the Cambridge Music Society. In 1847 he was ordained and spent most of his ministry in Durham.

He wrote more than 300 hymn tunes, many of which are still used, and sixty of them appeared in the first edition of the Church of England's hymnal, *Hymns Ancient and Modern*, issued in 1861. In addition to his composition of hymn tunes, Dykes published sermons and articles on religion and played the organ, piano, violin, and horn. Like Reginald Heber, his life was creative and brief. He died at the age of fifty-three.

In both its verse and its tune, "Holy, Holy, Holy" fills the believer with reverence and joy. In some ways, it's a paradoxical hymn. It can be sung loudly and with great gusto as a hymn of praise to our God who is "perfect in power, in love and purity." Or, it can be sung quietly as a hymn of awe and wonder to our God "who wert, and art, and evermore shall be." Impossible as it may be, perhaps it should be sung both ways. Such is the majesty and mystery of God.

Meditation

Can We Risk Being Merciful?

There are all kinds of memorable words in this grand hymn upon which we could meditate, but the words, "merciful and mighty," repeated in the first and final verses, keep coming back to me. Whenever I sing them, I remember Ruskin's description of truly great persons: "they see something divine in every other man and are endlessly, foolishly, and incredibly merciful."

Wonderful words, but would we dare live by them? We can sing that God is both merciful and mighty but, after all, God can afford to be merciful; when you're the "Lord God Almighty" you can take the risk of being foolishly merciful. You could risk living by Theodore Roosevelt's advice to "speak softly and carry a big stick" if you were as big as God, but the rest of us possess no such big club.

Of course, Jesus tried to live by this ethic of incredible mercy, but look where it landed him—on the cross! And even there, he persisted in being merciful, asking God to forgive his executioners because they "knew not what they were doing." But what good did it do him? They kept right on doing it.

Of course, we can exempt ourselves from this high and merciful ethic by noting that Jesus, after all, was doing a special job on the cross, a job that has not been assigned to us, that of dying for the sins of the world. That task is not required of us, so we don't have to be all that merciful. That was Jesus' job, not ours.

Thus, we can follow Teddy Roosevelt rather than Jesus and find the biggest stick available as we make our way through a hostile world. But Jesus didn't exempt us from the work of being merciful; in fact, he called us to such impossible work. He even promised that our works of mercy would be rewarded; he said that in being merciful we would receive mercy.

But if it didn't work for him (he still got crucified), how could it work for us? Did he mean that every deed of mercy will, in some reciprocal manner, be rewarded, and that on some future day when we need mercy, we'll receive it? I think he meant something much bigger than that.

In the early 1960s a sordid scandal rocked England and, eventually, resulted in the collapse of Prime Minister Harold Macmillan's government. At the heart of the mess was John Profumo, Secretary of State for War, whose brief affair with Christine Keeler was finally exposed, including the fact that

Keeler was also involved with a Russian spy. When it was all over, Profumo, who might have moved upward in the government, might even have become Prime Minister, was totally humiliated as a liar and adulterer who had betrayed his country, his wife and family, and his own promising career.

Understandably, he completely disappeared, never again seeking return to public office. Instead, unnoticed by those whose view of life is limited to the front pages, he spent the rest of his life at Toynbee Hall, a settlement house in the East End of London, where he washed dishes, cleaned toilets, visited prisons, and helped the poor.

By the end of his life, he had become President of Toynbee Hall and, when he died in 2006, the *Daily Telegraph* wrote, "No one in public life ever did more to atone for his sins; no one behaved with more silent dignity as his name was repeatedly dragged through the mud; and few ended their lives as loved and revered by those who knew him."

What kept him at those works of mercy over all those years? He certainly didn't "obtain mercy" as, every so often, the juicy old scandal would be warmed up again by some tabloid for those who feast upon such fetid fare. I suspect that he discovered that in doing the works of mercy, we come to realize that all of life is one great, mysterious web of merciful events, that God's mercy is the underlying reality of the world, and that to live mercifully is to live realistically.

There was a time when, on every Friday morning, I would drive to the heart of Detroit to pour coffee at a soup kitchen. Upon arriving at 7:30 a.m., a wreath of human wretchedness would encompass the door, awaiting the opening. "All sorts and conditions" of humankind would receive a hot meal and then drink coffee all morning, after having spent another night on the streets.

What had brought them to this condition? Sometimes it was the result of their choice, but what other circumstances brought them to that choice? And what other pure accidents happened along their way? It didn't take much imagination to realize that there was not much difference between us, that we were all the results of the big "if" factor in human experience, myself included.

What if I had not been assigned a seat in a high school biology class, a seat that placed me in front of a girl who invited me to attend her church? What if some more talented candidate had been called to my first church so that my ministry started elsewhere, from where a different set of "ifs" would have dictated my journey? Such "what if" experiences took place all along the way in my life and career, leading back to the really big one: what if my father had not met my mother, so that I had never been born?

I don't know why those homeless folks were homeless, nor do I know what greater mercy awaits in their eternal future. For that matter, I don't know why I never ended up in a soup kitchen, having some young pastor pouring coffee into my plastic cup.

All I know is that works of mercy restore our relationships with God's entire family, reminding us that we are not so much the result of our good choices, but that all of us, all along, have been receiving God's providential mercy.

All of life is about mercy. We can afford to take the risk of being merciful, of bearing one another's burdens, because we are at our strongest and safest when we are living fully as members of the entire human family, over which the loving providence of God is somehow mysteriously and mercifully working.

In the Cross of Christ I Glory

1. In the cross of Christ__ I glo - ry, to - wering
2. When the woes of life__ o'er - take me, hopes de -
3. When the sun of bliss__ is beam - ing light and
4. Bane and bles - sing, pain__ and plea - sure, by the
5. In the cross of Christ__ I glo - ry, to - wering

o'er the wrecks of time; all the light of
ceive, and fears an - noy, ne - ver shall the
love up - on my way, from the cross the
cross are sanc - ti - fied; peace is there that
o'er the wrecks of time; all the light of

sa - cred__ sto - ry ga - thers round its head su - blime.
cross__ for - sake me. Lo! it glows with peace and joy.
ra - diance stream-ing adds more lus - ter to the day.
knows__ no__ mea-sure, joys that through all time a - bide.
sa - cred__ sto - ry ga - thers round its head su - blime.

20

In the Cross of Christ I Glory

This hymn was written by a brilliant nineteenth-century poet and linguist, John Bowring, who lived eighty productive years from 1792 to 1872. During his lifetime he learned 200 languages and could carry out conversations in 100 of those. He was the editor of an influential journal, the *Westminster Review*, and he was appointed to several important political offices: commissioner to France, British consul at Hong Kong, and governor of Hong Kong. He also served as a political economist in the Netherlands and France.

He was twice elected as a member of Parliament, and Queen Victoria knighted him in 1854. In 1859 he and his family were poisoned while in China; his wife died but he survived. He returned to England and wrote extensively and lectured widely until his own death. He was a devout man and, given the centrality of the cross in this hymn, it is surprising that he was a member of the Unitarian Church.

Bowring's writings were voluminous—a total of thirty-six published volumes on politics, economics, biography, science, religion, and poetry. He translated writings from twenty-two languages. Two of his books contained sacred poetry, and two of those are in many hymnals: an Advent hymn, "Watchman, Tell Us of the Night," and this famous Lenten hymn.

On his extensive travels, he collected beetles; before his death, he presented his collection of more than 84,000 species to the British Museum.

While some doubt the authenticity of this story, the great hymnologist Erik Routley has described the background of "In the Cross of Christ I Glory":

"The first thing you see as you approach Macao (Island near Hong Kong) is the great white church of Our Lady of Fatima, perched on the island's highest hill. In a revolution the church was destroyed, save for the great west front. This west wall still stands, and crowning the topmost point is a great metal cross, which (in repeated attacks) has survived destruction. It was this cross, blackened with smoke, that inspired John Bowring's hymn."

Bowring asked that the first line of his hymn be engraved on his tombstone: "In the cross of Christ I glory, Towering o'er the wrecks of time."

The tune, "Rathbun," was composed in 1849 by an American, Ithamar Conkey, of Scottish ancestry. At that time, Conkey was the organist of the Central Baptist Church in Norwich, Connecticut. The circumstances surrounding the composing of the tune are touching.

One Sunday the preacher was preaching a series of sermons on "Words on the Cross," and he used the hymn, "In the Cross of Christ I Glory."

The weather was rainy, and only one member of the choir showed up. Conkey was so disappointed that he went home and composed a new tune for the hymn and dedicated it to the only member of the choir who appeared that Sunday. Her name was Mrs. Beriah S. Rathbun, a soprano soloist, and therefore the tune is "Rathbun."

Conkey went from Norwich to New York City, where he was bass soloist at Calvary Episcopal Church and then bass soloist and choir director of Madison Avenue Baptist Church.

The hymn is based on Galatians 6:14: "May I never boast of anything except the cross of our Lord Jesus Christ, by which the world has been crucified to me, and I to the world." It also has references to passages in 1 Corinthians 1 and 2. The text from Galatians is also the basis for Isaac Watts' famous hymn, "When I Survey the Wondrous Cross" (see pp. 49–53).

This Lenten hymn is a splendid example of Romantic poetry but has no morbidity. It fully acknowledges the significance of the cross, but it also affirms the victory of Christ through his resurrection. It is essentially a hymn of comfort to Christians in the midst of sorrow and trial and the triumph of Christ even on the cross. Pay special attention to the second stanza:

> When the woes of life o'er take me,
> Hopes deceive, and fears annoy,
> Never shall the cross forsake me:
> Lo! It glows with peace and joy.

It may have been intended for Lent, but "In the Cross of Christ I Glory" can be sung any day of the year.

Meditation

Bearing and Wearing the Cross

There is no way in which crucifixion can be beautified.

Most of you have heard or read a sufficient number of accounts about crucifixion to know that it was, in the words of Cicero, "the most cruel and disgusting penalty." It cannot be compared to any modern form of execution, whether by electric chair, lethal injection, firing squad, or the gallows, because it was a hideously torturous method of making a long, drawn out, excruciatingly painful public display of what would happen to those who opposed the iron will of the Roman Empire. It was Rome's way of saying, "This is what we will do to you if you question our power."

We must never picture three simple crosses mounted upon a hill against a glorious sunset. Crosses were placed along the most crowded roads where, close to the ground, spectators could hear the groans of the dying, smell the stench of death, or else, following death, witness the victims' bodies crawling with insects, ravaged by carrion, or torn by packs of hungry dogs. How odd that the cross should be turned into a piece of costume jewelry!

For whatever reason, I have never worn a cross as a sign of my faith or my clerical vocation. As far as I can remember, there was never a cross upon any of my liturgical vestments. This was not the result of any decision to be plain; it just happened that way.

There was, however, one cross that I did wear, and that was on my badge as a chaplain of the city fire department. As I recall, there was also one on the white helmet that I wore when summoned to a fire, as well as on the waterproof coat that indicated that I was the chaplain.

I was summoned only to the worst fires, those in which there was the devastating loss of a family's home, or those in which someone had died in the fire. On those DUA calls in which someone was "dead upon arrival," it was the chaplain's expected duty to accompany the firemen into and out of the building with the body. In such cases, the fire was sufficiently "under control," but still burning.

On at least one occasion, I climbed the ladder with the firemen (the dead were often on the second floor), proceeded through a window to the location of the body, and then led the firemen carrying the body out of the building. I'm not sure what the chaplain's presence signified to the firemen, most of whom were Roman Catholic, but it was a very necessary ritual for them.

For some reason, the presence of the man wearing the cross brought comfort and strength amidst the scene of wreckage and death. I don't remember ever thinking of it as an instance in which the cross was "towering o'er the wrecks of time," although it was a very real demonstration of that truth.

The same was true even when there was the loss of a home, but without any death. The family would be in a nearby car, shivering in colder weather, and my duty would be to speak some simple word of comfort to their benumbing loss. There was no way in which they could identify my denomination by the mark of the cross on the rough vestments worn by a fire chaplain. Again, all they seemed to need was the man wearing the cross.

Of course, the greatest wreckage over which the cross towers is that of the Roman Empire. The "glory that was Rome" is long gone, but what remains all over the face of the earth are millions of churches, both large and small, which, despite their disunity and differences, all display a cross.

How utterly amazing that Jesus took a symbol of imperial power and cruelty, and transformed it into a symbol of hope and victory. The cross carries different meanings for different folks. Some "cross themselves" during prayer and worship (even during athletic contests!), others genuflect in reverence before the cross on a high altar, while others simply gaze upon its "radiance streaming."

But finally, that cruel cross was emptied of its terror and transformed into the very heart of our message to the world. When Paul's brilliant sermon on Mars Hill in Athens (Acts 17) failed to convince a sophisticated audience, he came down to Corinth, where he distilled his message to single sentence, "I decided to know nothing among you except Jesus Christ, and him crucified" (1 Cor 2:2).

I turned in my fireman's helmet and "vestments" many years ago. I'm not even steady on a step ladder these days. All I have left is my badge. But I hope that the way I live on every ordinary day will always somehow tell the world that I'm still "the man wearing the cross."

O Worship the King

1 O wor - ship the King all - glo - rious a - bove,
2 O tell of his might and sing of his grace,
3 Your boun - ti - ful care, what tongue can re - cite?
4 Frail chil - dren of dust, and fee - ble as frail,
5 O mea - sure - less Might, un - change - a - ble Love,

O grate - ful - ly sing his power and his love:
whose robe is the light, whose can - o - py space.
It breathes in the air, it shines in the light;
in you do we trust, nor find you to fail.
whom an - gels de - light to wor - ship a - bove!

our shield and de - fend - er, the An - cient of Days,
His char - iots of wrath the deep thun - der - clouds form,
it streams from the hills, it de - scends to the plain,
Your mer - cies, how ten - der, how firm to the end,
Your ran - somed cre - a - tion, with glo - ry a - blaze,

pa - vil - ioned in splen - dor and gird - ed with praise.
and dark is his path on the wings of the storm.
and sweet - ly dis - tills in the dew and the rain.
our Mak - er, De - fend - er, Re - deem - er, and Friend!
in true ad - o - ra - tion shall sing to your praise!

21

O Worship the King

This hymn is based on Psalm 104, but it is a meditation on it, not a versification or paraphrase of it.

Psalm 104 begins:

Bless the Lord, O my soul.
> O Lord my God, you are very great
You are clothed with honor and majesty,
> Wrapped in light as with a garment.
You stretch out the heavens like a tent,
> You set the beams of your chambers on the waters,
> You make the clouds your chariot,
> You ride on the wings of the wind,
You make the winds your messengers,
> Fire and flame your ministers.

The Psalm is a creation Psalm, praising God for God's power and majesty in creating the world and all that it is in.

It was written by Robert Grant, who was born in India to Scottish parents in 1779, and died in India in 1838. He was educated at Cambridge University, admitted to the bar in 1807, and elected to Parliament in 1808. He was a leader in the effort to abolish slavery in England, and in 1833 he successfully advocated for his bill in Parliament that removed civil restrictions on Jews in England.

He also served with distinction as the governor of Bombay for four years and was knighted in 1834. As governor of Bombay, he was an advocate for the poor and sought to alleviate their suffering. The residents of India considered him their friend, and today there is a medical college in India named after him—the second oldest medical school in the nation.

He was one of the evangelical leaders in the Church of England and a strong proponent of the missionary movement. His hymn texts were published in various places during his lifetime and collected and published posthumously by his brother.

The composer of the tune, Lyons, is a matter of debate. It first appeared in a hymnbook published in 1815, under the attribution "Subject Haydn." But it's not known whether this was Franz Josef Haydn or his younger brother Johann Michael Haydn.

Other recent research credits the hymn to a German composer, Michael Kraus, who resided in Sweden but traveled extensively in Europe. It now seems likely that Kraus was the composer. He was a gifted musician who wrote operas and many instrumental works. Franz Josef Haydn said that he was "one of the greatest geniuses I have met."

This is a joyous hymn with two opening phrases of praise, followed by a more somber third phrase, and then a triumphant final phrase. As powerful as this hymn is as a hymn celebrating God's creation to the world, it also has a pastoral dimension, which is the heart of virtually all great hymn writing. Amidst God's glory and power, it identifies those in distress and offers solace and comfort.

For all of us who carry heavy burdens, for all of us weighed down with care, consider these lines:

Frail children of dust, and feeble as frail,
In Thee do we trust, nor find Thee to fail;
Thy mercies how tender, how firm to the end,
Our maker, defender, redeemer, and friend.

Meditation

My Spiritual Neighbors

"Thy bountiful care what tongue can recite . . ."

My guess is that most of my neighbors have never sung the lovely fourth verse of this hymn. It appears that most of them don't attend worship, because it's very quiet around here when I leave for church on Sunday morning. Maybe they "did church" when they were growing up, but now do their praying at home. Or maybe they take their Sabbath rest with the Sunday newspaper, along with their bacon and eggs, or just sleep in.

I don't spend much time thinking about what they're doing; besides, it's none of my business. Then too, they're a pretty diverse bunch. A few of them started their lives in other countries such as Germany, Norway, Wales, Vietnam, Mexico, or El Salvador. Most are married, while others are single, divorced, widowed, or gay/lesbian.

A few of them don't like one another, but most of us get along fairly well. The friendliest neighbors are the dogs, but I don't know anything about their religious preferences.

However, let me make it clear that all my neighbors are "spiritual" people, although not in the sense that we usually use that term. I say that because 99 percent of the conversations I have with them center upon a spiritual matter.

Every night before sundown, I pedal as fast as I can around the neighborhood for 9.3 miles (15,000 meters) for my daily exercise. However, I always stop for a few minutes to chat with one or two of my neighbors, and whenever we do, we always talk about that very spiritual subject: the weather.

We all agree with what Jesus said about the weather, even those who've never read the New Testament. We all know that the daily weather is proof of God's "unconditional, positive regard" for all people. We might not use those words of Carl

Rogers to express our theology of the weather; however, whatever the weather on a given day, none of us are excluded from its benefits.

When it rains, it rains on all of us. When the sun shines, it shines on all of us. Even if the rain falls on our planned picnic, we know it's good for the earth. Even when we complain about the heat and humidity, we know that it keeps our flowers blooming and our plants growing.

No one gets left behind or left out by the weather. According to Jesus, that's why we must love one another, especially those we define as our enemies. What he said was that we should love our enemies, even those who persecute us, because of the stubborn fact that our heavenly Father somehow finds a way to treat all of us with the same unconditional and inescapable goodness. God "makes his sun rise on the evil and the good, and sends rain on the righteous and on the unrighteous" (Matt 5:45).

Theologians use a special word to describe this infuriating and inclusive behavior of God; they call it grace, by which they describe the unmerited, inescapable love that somehow includes all of us. Grace means that we can no more escape God's love than we can escape the weather.

Just as we can't decide that it's not a rainy day and opt out of it, neither can we decide to opt out of God's all-inclusive love. For some mysterious reason, God loves the very people I can't stand, just as some of them can't stand me. But God can somehow stand all of us—and even love us unconditionally!

There was once a time when one of our neighbors whom we liked said that another neighbor was "evil." So we decided to invite that evil neighbor to dinner. We had a wonderful evening with him and his wife and discovered that this "evil" man had done many things in his life that were kind and tender-hearted. Apparently, the other neighbor who described this man as evil hadn't been listening to what the weather is always trying to teach us.

George MacDonald, the nineteenth-century preacher and writer who was the spiritual mentor of C. S. Lewis, wrote that the miracles of Jesus were "small and swift" demonstrations of what God is always doing in a larger, slower way. When Jesus turned water into wine, or caused bread to multiply suddenly, he was showing us what our loving God is always doing for all of us: employing the elements to work together with the weather to grow grapes or wheat or whatever food we need.

In this way, God's care "breathes in the air, shines in the light, streams from the hills, descends to the plain, and sweetly distills in the dew and the rain." In this sense, all weather is good weather. Whatever today's weather, it is telling us, as Huston Smith wrote so beautifully, that "we are in good hands, and in gratitude for that fact we do well to bear one another's burdens."

Savior, Like a Shepherd Lead Us

1. Sa - vior, like a shep-herd lead us, Much we need Thy ten - der care;
2. We are Thine, do Thou be - friend us, Be the guar-dian of our way;
3. Thou hast pro-mised to re - ceive us, Poor and sin - ful though we be;
4. Ear - ly let us seek Thy fa - vour, Ear - ly let us do Thy will;

In Thy plea - sant pas-tures feed us, For our use Thy folds pre - pare:
Keep Thy flock, from sin de - fend us, Seek us when we go as - tray:
Thou hast mer - cy to re - lieve us, Grace to cleanse, and pow'r to free:
Bles - sed Lord and on - ly Sa - viour, With Thy love our bo-soms fill:

Bles-sèd Je - sus, bles-sèd Je - sus, Thou hast bought us, Thine we are;
Bles-sèd Je - sus, bles-sèd Je - sus, Hear, O hear us when we pray;
Bles-sèd Je - sus, bles-sèd Je - sus, Ear - ly let us turn to Thee;
Bles-sèd Je - sus, bles-sèd Je - sus, Thou hast loved us, love us still;

Bles-sèd Je - sus, bles-sèd Je - sus, Thou hast bought us, Thine we are.
Bles-sèd Je - sus, bles-sèd Je - sus, Hear, O hear us when we pray.
Bles-sèd Je - sus, bles-sèd Je - sus, Ear - ly let us turn to Thee.
Bles-sèd Je - sus, bles-sèd Je - sus, Thou hast loved us, love us still.

22

Savior, Like a Shepherd Lead Us

This is a beautiful hymn of God's presence and consolation. The author of the hymn is listed as Dorothy Ann Thrupp because it came from her hymnbook, *Hymns for the Young*, published in 1836. In actual fact, we don't know exactly who composed this hymn, but let's assume it was Dorothy Ann Thrupp, because she was a creative and prolific contributor to hymnody.

She was born in 1779 in London and died there in 1847. In addition to her editing the book of hymns for young people, she wrote many other hymns—chiefly for children—and they were widely published during her lifetime. She was also the author of many religious essays designed for children.

Despite her many achievements in behalf of ministry to children, that is about all we know about Dorothy Ann Thrupp. She steadfastly avoided publicity in her own lifetime.

Perhaps not surprisingly, we know a lot more about the male composer of the tune. He is William Batchelder Bradbury, who was born in Maine in 1816 and died in New Jersey in 1868.

Bradbury was a music machine. During the peak of his productivity from 1841–1867, he produced more than two collections of music a year and fifty-nine books during his lifetime. One collection, *The Jubilee*, sold a quarter of a million copies—a stupendous amount for music, then or now. He and his brother founded the Bradbury Piano Company, which later became part of the Knabe Piano Company.

He was educated in music in Boston, New York City, England, and Germany. He settled for most of his life in New York City, where he taught, conducted musical gatherings, composed, and edited music books.

He earned lasting fame as the composer of the tune to "Jesus Loves Me." His lucid, unadorned tunes paved the way for gospel music.

The simplicity of this hymn is obvious, and the fact that it was written for children is evident in the second stanza:

> Blessed Jesus, blessed Jesus,
> Early let us turn to Thee;
> Blessed Jesus, blessed Jesus,
> Early let us turn to Thee.

Whether early or late, the call rings true to all of us: "Let us turn to Thee."

Meditation

What Didn't Happen Today

Whenever I hear this hymn, there's a story about it that I can never forget. I'm not even sure if the story is true; it sounds so much like a stock, sentimental pulpit story. I have since, however, found two confirmations of its authenticity.

Maybe the reason why this story made such an impression on my mind is because I was a teenager when I first heard it at the weekly Sunday afternoon evangelistic meeting of the Schenectady City Mission.

The preacher that afternoon was a gifted pianist whose message was presented by the playing of selected gospel hymns, one of which was this hymn, a particular favorite of Ira D. Sankey (1840–1908), song leader for the famous evangelist D. L. Moody. The story goes like this.

On Christmas Eve 1875, when Sankey was traveling on a Delaware River steamboat, some of the passengers asked him to sing one of his own hymns for which he was famous. He sang, instead, one of his favorites but composed by another author, *Savior, Like a Shepherd Lead Us.*

When he had finished singing, one of the passengers, recognizing him from a newspaper photo, stepped forward and asked him an odd question. He asked if he had ever served in the Union Army. Sankey had, indeed, been a member of the Twelfth Pennsylvania Regiment, responding in 1860 to Lincoln's call for volunteers.

The stranger then asked an even more provocative question, whether Sankey remembered a moonlit night in 1862 when he was doing picket duty. Sankey did remember that night, but could never have suspected what he was about to hear.

The man then told Sankey of how, on that bright night, he was also on duty as a sniper in the Confederate army, concealed in the shadows, with his rifle aimed at Sankey, a perfect target in clear moonlight. Just as he was ready to pull the trigger, Sankey raised his voice and began to sing the words, "Savior, like a shepherd lead us," a song the sniper remembered his mother often singing to him. He could not pull the trigger and allowed the enemy soldier, Sankey, to live.

Of course, this is a wonderful story for the pulpiteer, one that a preacher can embellish by supplying the dramatic, inner thoughts of both Sankey and the sniper. But I don't remember it being told with such homiletical melodrama; I remember the simple, unadorned story, and the preacher/pianist then sitting down to play it for us in that rather shabby mission chapel.

I was the only teenager in the tiny congregation. The rest were the faithful few elderly supporters of the mission, a few drunks who had been brought in from the mission dormitory to hear the gospel, and the mission superintendent, a dear old Swede who had taken an interest in me and who prayed for me daily during my college years.

What I didn't know on that afternoon, and would realize only after many years of my journey, was the truth of those opening words, and how "much we need Thy tender care." It is only by looking back to that afternoon and that hymn that I can now, in my latter years, only begin to imagine of how many bad things *didn't* happen to me, and how many times I escaped dangers of which I am completely unaware.

The only times when I come even near to such a realization are when, for example, speeding along an Interstate highway at an excessive speed, I suddenly pass by the scene of a serious accident on the other side of the median and realize how the sudden turn of some stranger's steering wheel could have placed me in the same, life-threatening peril. And how many other times during an "average" day am I completely oblivious to the same marvelous deliverance? Indeed, are there any "average" days?

And so, in remembering that Sunday afternoon many years ago, the preacher/pianist, the simple gospel hymn, the odd crowd of saints and sinners gathered in that mission chapel, and my early born-again faith which would be tested, stretched, restored, and renewed over the years, I am grateful for all the things that haven't happened to me, for all the secret, mighty acts of God of which I was never aware.

Maybe you'll join me at the end of every day with the simple prayer, "Lord, we thank you for what could have, . . . but didn't happen today."

Just As I Am, Without One Plea

23

Just As I Am, Without One Plea

We know this hymn was written by a woman, and the author is the remarkable Charlotte Elliott, who lived a long life of eighty-two fruitful years from 1789 to 1871. She was born in Clapham, England and died in Brighton. At the age of thirty-two, she was stricken with illness that left her a semi-invalid for the rest of her life.

About her illness, she wrote, "My Heavenly Father knows, and He alone, what it is, day after day, and hour after hour, to fight against bodily feelings of almost overpowering weakness and languor and exhaustion; to resolve as He enables me to do, not to yield to the slothfulness, the depression, the irritability, such as a body causes me to long to indulge, but to rise every morning determined on taking this for my motto, 'If any man will come after me, let him deny himself, take up his cross daily, and follow me.' "

A year after she was stricken, she found herself amidst a spiritual crisis and told the evangelist Henri Cesar Malan that she did not know how to come to Christ. He told her, "Why not come *just as you are*? You have only to come to Him *just as you are.*"

She considered that day her spiritual birthday and observed it every year. Twelve years later as she reflected on his words and as she watched helplessly as her family prepared for a charity event, she penned "Just As I Am" as a statement of her faith.

Writing hymns was one way that Charlotte Elliott combated her pain and depression, and she "is given the foremost place among English women hymnwriters." She wrote approximately

150 hymns, many of which reflect her chronic pain and illness but also reflect her faith that gave her perseverance and hope.

It is striking that during most of her lifetime, "Just As I Am" was published widely in books and pamphlets, and, at her request, it appeared anonymously.

Her hymns were collected and published in several collections, including her *Invalid's Hymn Book*, which went through several editions over twenty years (1834–1854), *Hours of Sorrow Cheered and Comforted* (1836), *Hymns for a Week* (1839), and *Thoughts in Verse on Sacred Subjects* (1869).

The composer of the tune, "Woodworth," is William Batchelder Bradbury (see pp. 159–60).

"Just As I Am" has been widely translated and brought consolation to millions. The hymn was always published with her choice of John 6:37 as the text: "Him that cometh to me I will in no wise cast out." After Elliott died, more than a thousand letters of gratitude for this hymn were found among her papers.

The knowledgeable hymnologist James Davidson wrote about Elliott, "Though weak and feeble in body, she possessed a strong imagination and a well-cultured and intellectual mind. . . . For those in sickness and in sorrow, she has sung as few others have done."

At one point, her physician visited her and gave her a pamphlet containing "Just as I Am." Because of her insistence on anonymity, her name was not attached to it. Unknowingly, he told her, "I know that this will please you."

Her own brother declared, "In the course of a long ministry I hope I have been permitted to see some fruit for my labours; but I feel far more has been done by a single hymn of my sister's."

It has been, of course, the theme hymn for the Billy Graham crusades, and Graham used it for the title of his autobiography, *Just as I Am*. About the hymn, Graham has written, "In coming to Christ we should not wait until we have straightened out our lives a bit. No small improvement we can effect will make us any more acceptable to Him. God loves us just as we are and we should come that way."

As Graham issued his many calls to come forward, thousands if not millions of people have answered his summons, singing:

> Just as I am, though tossed about
> With many a conflict, many a doubt,
> Fightings and fears within, without,
> O Lamb of God, I come, I come.

Who among us cannot sing this hymn?

Meditation

Just the Way You Are

In the little room in which I write these meditations, someone is always smiling at me. On the bookcase in back of me is the last birthday card that I received from my friend, Fred Rogers, Mister Rogers. I don't want to give the impression that we were special friends, because everyone Fred knew was a special friend. However, once we had met, Fred always remembered my birthday because we were born in the same month of the same year, but ten days apart.

On the front of the card is Fred's smiling face. He is wearing his traditional zipper-front sweater and the usual necktie, and he is putting on his sneakers. On the top of the card are his words, "I like you just the way you are." That thought is finished inside the card with the words, "No one else can fill your sneakers!"

From what I know about Fred's faith, I think those words pretty well express his theology of radical grace. However, the millions of children who heard Fred repeat those words would not have realized that they were listening to a theological statement. My guess is that most adults also understand them the same way, not as a formulation of Fred's faith, but as a loving affirmation that little children need to hear over and over again as they struggle with the wonder and worry of growing up.

It takes a huge stretch of one's theological imagination to believe that God feels that way about us. "Yes, Jesus loves me, the Bible tells me so," and we have all kinds of proof texts therein to support that claim. There's no problem in believing that God loves me, but it takes a giant leap of faith to believe that *the God who loves me also likes me.*

After all, I don't even like myself, and I don't know too many normal, healthy people who fully do like themselves. Of course, we all know a few people who are fully pleased with themselves, and it's not much fun being around them, because they are actually, egotistically satisfied with their exaggerated self-image.

No, I don't like myself just as I am, and I can't believe that God does either. I have lots of work to do on myself before I could ever take Fred's words seriously as a theological truth. Great words for little kids, but not for me!

Even though I've been struggling up the steep hill of self-improvement for my entire life, I still don't like myself, just the way I am. But what if God does? What if God sees something going on in me of which I am totally unaware?

The Apostle Paul thought that God does see something that is good and likeable in us; God sees something deep within us that is worth working on. Paul wanted us to keep working on ourselves, doing the best we can to do God's will and live like the children of God; however, Paul insisted that God is the main artist in our re-creation as genuine children of God.

He wrote to the Philippians, "work out your own salvation with fear and trembling, for it is God who is at work in you, enabling you both to will and to work for his own good pleasure" (Phil 2:12, 13). Undergirding our own decisions and doings is God's own deciding and doing. God is the One who is working on us, even if we are unaware of what is happening.

As a master woodcarver, God sees something in the human block of wood that the rest of can't see. The chiseling and carving may take many years as God works at defining the true heart of our being, the perfect image that God sees in us.

Some of God's working may be painful. Indeed, our own failures may be part of the necessary process until God's image is formed in us. Robert Frost spoke of them as "mistakes made by the selves we had to be, not able to be, perhaps, what we wished, or what looking back half the time it seems we could so easily have been, or ought."

Along the way, there will be days when the climbing seems effortless, but also other days when we slide backwards down the steep mountainside. But God is going to finish the work. "The one who calls you is faithful, and he will do this" (1 Thess 5:24).

So remember the words of François Fénelon, "Do not be discouraged at your faults; bear with yourself in correcting them, as you would with your neighbor."

At the end of every day, remember that God likes you, likes the lovely person that God sees in you and is working to complete—and God is doing this in every human life!

Come, Ye Thankful People, Come

1. Come, ye thank-ful peo-ple, come, raise the song of harv-est home; all is safe-ly ga - thered in, ere the win-ter storms be - gin. God our Ma - ker doth pro - vide for our wants to be sup-plied; come to God's own tem - ple, come, raise the song of harv-est home.

2. All the world is God's own field, fruit as praise to God we yield; wheat and tares to - ge - ther sown are to joy or sor - row grown; first the blade and then the ear, then the full corn shall ap - pear; Lord of harv - est, grant that we whole - some grain and pure may be.

3. For the Lord our God shall come, and shall take the harv-est home; from the field shall in that day all of - fen - ses purge a - way, gi - ving an-gels charge at last in the fire the tares to cast; but the fruit - ful ears to store in the gar - ner e - ver - more.

4. E - ven so, Lord, quick - ly come, bring thy fi - nal harv - est home; ga - ther thou thy peo - ple in, free from sor - row, free from sin, there, for - e - ver pu - ri - fied, in thy pre - sence to a - bide; come, with all thine an - gels, come, raise the glo - rious harv - est home.

24

Come, Ye Thankful
People, Come

This is one of the best hymns of gratitude ever written, and it appears frequently in Thanksgiving services.

It contains three stanzas focusing largely on the fruits of creation and concludes with a stirring stanza about the great heavenly harvest yet to come.

The hymn was written for village harvest festivals in England. It uses the agrarian imagery of the gospels: the growing seed (from Mark 4) and the tares among the wheat (in Matthew 13).

"Come, Ye Thankful People, Come" was written by Henry Alford, who was born in London in 1810 and died in Canterbury in 1871. His was a family of clergy; he was the sixth generation of Anglican priests. He was educated at Cambridge and was ordained in 1833. In 1857 he was appointed Dean of Canterbury Cathedral, a post he held until his death. Alford wrote this hymn during his service in a rural parish where the fall harvest festival was a significant occasion and where the failure of a crop meant financial ruin.

Alford was a child prodigy. When he was six, he wrote a biography of the Apostle Paul, and before he was ten he composed several Latin odes, a history of the Jews, and a series of sermon outlines. When he was ten, he published a pamphlet, entitled *Looking Unto Jesus: The Believers' Support Under Trials and Afflictions*. At age eleven, he put together his first hymnbook.

When he was sixteen, he dedicated his life to God on the flyleaf of his Bible, where he wrote, "I do this day, in the presence of God and my own soul, renew my covenant with God, and solemnly determine henceforth to become his, and to do his work as far as in me lies."

He became a renowned biblical scholar and wrote a four-volume commentary on the Greek New Testament. Alford labored over it for twenty years, and it became a standard work in the field. He was also a prodigious poem and hymn writer, publishing two volumes of his poetry and a hymnbook. He also edited the poems of John Donne and translated Homer's *Odyssey*.

One of his colleagues said of him: "I really think he was morally the bravest man I ever knew. His perfect purity of mind and singleness of purpose seemed to give him confidence and unobtrusive self-respect which never failed him." He chose his own Latin epitaph for his gravestone, which translated into English is: "The inn of a traveler on his way to Jerusalem."

At the conclusion to a hard day's work and at the end of a meal, Alford was known to stand and then offer a prayer of thanksgiving to God.

The tune is "St. George's Windsor," composed by George J. Elvey, who was also a child prodigy. Elvey began his study of the organ under the organist at Canterbury Cathedral. At the age of nineteen he applied for—and received—appointment as the organist of St. George's Chapel in Windsor Castle, surpassing many famous and established musicians in England.

He educated several members of the royal family and was knighted in 1871.

This tune was attached to "Come, Ye Thankful People, Come" almost from the beginning when they were united in the Church of England's famous hymnal, *Hymns Ancient and Modern*, published in 1861. As is often the case, Elvey originally composed the tune for another hymn, before it was linked to "Come, Ye Thankful People, Come." Alford named the hymn in honor of the chapel in Windsor Castle where he served as organist for an astonishing forty-seven years.

Throughout his career, Elvey wrote many anthems, two oratorios, and compositions for the organ.

An excellent spiritual exercise or spiritual discipline is making a gratitude list—identifying the things for which you are grateful. I've discovered it's one of the best antidotes to a number of ills that plague my spiritual life.

Singing "Come, Ye Thankful People, Come" can be the beginning of a gratitude list, and I'd encourage you to make such a list—either in your head or on paper. I think you'll be thankful for the result.

Meditation

Come Quickly!

I can almost smell the turkey roasting in the oven as I hum this hymn to myself. All kinds of Thanksgiving Day associations flood my mind, almost crowding out the words of the hymn.

Most people will hear the hymn's music as background for some TV program or ad on this day. Nowadays few churches have morning services on Thanksgiving Day; not that many people turn out for worship with so much else going on. Some churches, however, join with others for a community service on the night before, but even these may not be well-attended.

What's in your mind as you sing or hear this hymn? The old folks remember stories about the Plymouth pilgrims that were told in public school as we approached this holiday, or how we made a turkey with a potato as its body. Others who grew up after World War II will picture a Norman Rockwell family table.

But even those images are passing away. In the afternoon we'll watch football; the Detroit Lions always play on that day. Besides all of that, Thanksgiving Day has become the kick-off of the entire holiday season. Christmas decorations are already up in our malls, and tomorrow will be one of the great shopping orgies of the year.

So if we even sing this traditional song of the day, our memories and images will probably distract us from noticing that this hymn carries us far beyond Plymouth and all the other Thanksgiving Days since then.

We'll fail to notice that the words are leading us to reflect upon the return of the Lord, the coming of God, and the Day of Judgment—and that's certainly enough to spoil our Thanksgiving dinner and cast a dark cloud over our otherwise glittering holiday season. Just listen to some of those words as they call the Lord to "quickly come" and speak of the separation of the wholesome grain from the tares.

So what does a Thanksgiving table of such indigestible fare suggest to you?

If your early diet was based upon the Scofield Reference Bible and its clearly defined schedule of apocalyptic events, you'll be thinking of the rapture and the *Left Behind* movie scenes attached to those timetables.

If your theological diet was more "liberal," you will read such imagery as the way in which the ancients expressed their faith in the final victory of God, so that such images are taken generally but not literally.

Either way, fundamentalist or liberal, hardly any of us are longing for the Lord to "quickly come." After all, we've got our work to do, our dreams to pursue, our life to live. The Day of the Lord is for some future generation, after we've had our time. Why rush it by asking for the Lord to "quickly come"?

But one word of Paul cuts through the various apocalyptic scenarios and makes me pray that the restoration of all things will come ASAP. It's that little sentence tucked away toward the end of one of Paul's loftiest passages: "Now I know only in part; *then I will know fully, even as I have been fully known.*"

Whatever the final fireworks may be, I long for the day when I will meet my Lord and, in that moment, *finally meet myself*. What inexpressible joy to be fully and fairly known, to receive a full and fair performance review, to know why I did what I did, how I won a few and lost a few but how, despite it all, I will be fully loved and promoted to the next grade to learn my yet unlearned lessons, going on from strength to strength in the life of perfect service in God's heavenly kingdom.

Isn't that what judgment really means when we think of it as standing before the One who is both merciful and mighty? It means to be lovingly evaluated and sent onward to learn and become what we were always meant to become.

Why wouldn't anyone wish for such a restoration of all things for oneself and for all of God's children? If that's the kind of harvest that's coming, I have serious business to be about on every day. I'll have little time to go about judging others, trying to separate the wheat from the tares. After all, that's God's business, not mine. I'd better tend my own field as I get ready for my finals. I may not even have time to watch the Lions' game if I work on becoming "wholesome grain" for God's harvest.

Sometimes the poets say it best, so here's what, I think, awaits all of us, whether on a future day of judgment or upon our own final day.

Poet/farmer Wendell Berry described it this way: "I imagine the dead waking, dazed, into the shadowless light in which they know themselves altogether for the first time. It is a light that is merciless until they can accept its mercy; by it they are at once condemned and redeemed. It is Hell until it is Heaven. Seeing themselves in that light, if they are willing, they see how far they have failed the only justice of loving one another; it punishes them by their own judgment. And yet, in suffering that light's awful clarity, in seeing themselves within it, they see its forgiveness and its beauty, and are consoled. In it they are loved completely, even as they have been, and so are changed into what they could not have been but what, if they could have imagined it, they would have wished to be."

Even so, Lord, quickly come!

Abide With Me

1 A - bide with me: fast falls the ev - en - tide;
2 Swift to its close ebbs out life's lit - tle day;
3 I need your pres - ence ev - ery pass - ing hour.
4 I fear no foe with you at hand to bless,
5 Hold now your Word be - fore my clo - sing eyes.

the dark - ness deep - ens; Lord, with me a - bide.
earth's joys grow dim, its glo - ries pass a - way.
What but your grace can foil the tempt - er's power?
though ills have weight, and tears their bit - ter - ness.
Shine through the gloom and point me to the skies.

When o - ther help - ers fail and com - forts flee,
Change and de - cay in all a - round I see.
Who like your - self my guide and strength can be?
Where is death's sting? Where, grave, your vic - to - ry?
Heaven's morn - ing breaks and earth's vain shad - ows flee;

Help of the help - less, O a - bide with me.
O Lord who chang - es not, a - bide with me.
Through cloud and sun - shine, O a - bide with me.
I tri - umph still, if you a - bide with me.
in life, in death, O Lord, a - bide with me.

178

25

Abide With Me

This hymn is rarely sung today because it is associated with evening worship services. And yet, in my collection of CDs of hymns, I've discovered that it is nearly always one of the featured selections. In fact, it is sometimes called "the most popular hymn in the English language." It is based on the appearance of Christ on the road to Emmaus, where the two disciples say to Jesus: "Abide with us: for it is toward evening and the day is far spent" (Luke 24:29).

Despite that Scriptural origin, people misunderstand this hymn. It is actually about death—the end of life, not the end of day. It was written by Henry Francis Lyte, a very significant nineteenth-century hymn writer. In addition to "Abide With Me," Lyte is known for soaring hymns, including the beautiful "Praise, My Soul, the King of Heaven."

Lyte was born in Scotland in 1793 and orphaned at an early age. Educated at Trinity College, Dublin, he intended to become a doctor but was called into the ministry and ordained in the Church of England in 1815. He served only small parishes and his longest and last pastorate was in a poor church of fisherfolk in Devonshire. In his later years he suffered from tuberculosis and sought relief by visiting the beaches of the French Riviera. He died at Nice en route to Italy in 1847 at the age of only fifty-three.

In 1818 when he was twenty-five, Lyte reached a turning point when he struggled to deal with the death of a friend and fellow pastor. "I was greatly affected by the whole matter," he wrote, "and brought to look at life and its issue with a different eye than before; and I began to study my Bible, and preach in another manner than I had previously done."

Lyte was a gifted poet, which was recognized while he was a student when he won three poetry prizes. He published three books of his hymns and poems, including this gorgeous hymn, "Abide With Me."

There are two stories about how Lyte wrote this hymn. One records that Lyte composed it after attending to a good friend who was dying. During his last hours, the friend said quietly, "Abide with me. Abide with me." Possibly this was the death of Lyte's good friend early in his ministry.

Another version, which comes from a contemporary newspaper report, says that Lyte composed this hymn on his last Sunday in the pulpit. His gardener recalled, "After tea on that last Sunday, Lyte walked in the valley garden in front of the home, then down to the rocks, where he sat and composed. It was a lovely sunny day and the sun was setting over distant Dartmoor in a blaze of glory. On the left lay Brixham harbor like a pool of molten gold, with its picturesque trawling vessels lying peacefully at anchor. After the sun had set, Lyte returned to his study. His family thought he was resting, but he was putting the finishing touches to his immortal hymn."

He died in France three weeks later, pointing upward and whispering, "Peace! Joy!"

The tune, "Eventide," was written by a great nineteenth-century English musician, William Henry Monk. He was the editor of the Church of England's landmark hymnal, *Hymns Ancient and Modern*, which sold sixty million copies.

Monk was born and died in London. For nearly forty years he was music director at St. Matthias, Stoke Newington, London, and he also served as choirmaster and organist at King's College, London, for many years and as professor at the National Training School for Music. He was a high churchman and adapted plainchant for use in Anglican worship.

He completed his work on *Hymns Ancient and Modern* the day before he died, and his influence on this landmark in hymnology was so great it was often referred to as "Monk's Book."

There are two fascinating stories about Monk's composition of "Eventide." One recounts that he was in a hymnal committee meeting and realized that there wasn't a good tune for "Abide With Me." When the committee recessed for a while, Monk wrote the hymn in ten minutes. His concentration was reportedly so intense that a student sat six feet away practicing the piano and did not disturb him.

The second story comes from his wife, who said he wrote the hymn in a time of personal sorrow as they watched a glorious sunset together.

One scholar has concluded, "There can be no doubt that the tune had much to do with making 'Abide With Me' one of the best-known and best-loved hymns of the English-speaking peoples."

"Abide With Me" is played daily by the bells at Lyte's former parish, All Saints in Devonshire. It was sung at the wedding of King George VI, at the wedding of his daughter, the future Queen Elizabeth II, and at the funeral of Mother Teresa of Calcutta. It has been recorded by a variety of artists, including Paul McCartney of the Beatles, and it is played each year at the opening of the Rugby League Challenge Cup final in England.

Before Lyte's last service, those close to him urged him to rest, rather than preach. He responded, "It is better to wear out than to rust out." In that last sermon, Lyte declared, "O brethren, I stand here among you today, as alive from the dead, if I may hope to impress it upon you, and induce you to prepare for that solemn hour which must come to all, by a timely acquaintance with, appreciation of, and dependence on the death of Christ."

Then he wrote "Abide With Me," a prayer for God's presence in trial and at the end of life, which concludes,

Hold Thou Thy cross before my closing eyes;
Shine through the gloom and point me to the skies:
Heaven's morning breaks, and earth's vain shadows flee;
In life, in death, O Lord, abide with me.

In truth, we are all dying, but we don't have to be near death to utter Lyte's beautiful prayer.

Meditation

Sunrise, Sunset

H ere's a hymn for bedtime on every night of your life. Of course, if you're young you may not think you'll be needing it until later on in life. Those closing words about "Heaven's morning breaks, and earth's vain shadows flee" can make this seem like a hymn for old folks as they draw near to the end. As a matter of fact, it is sometimes sung at funerals.

But before you put this hymn on hold for your retirement years, think about some of its other words like, for example, "Swift to its close ebbs out life's little day."

Do you realize how swiftly our life is moving, even faster than we realize? In one of my favorite prayerbooks I read, "the days hasten on and we hasten with them." High speed Internet and other digital devices have convinced some of us that it is moving faster than in the olden days; however, that can be deceiving.

Life has always been moving too fast for humans; indeed, it was moving even faster back in 1847 when this hymn was written. Without our time-saving devices, a day was functionally even shorter for our great grandparents.

The Old Farmer's Almanac has stated that "no technology devised by man has been capable of altering the duration of the minutes, hours, days, weeks, months, and years that are for many people life's most precious commodity. Time can be managed, filled, passed, planned, saved, spent, lost, occasionally found, and, tragically, wasted, but it cannot be stretched, slowed, sped up, or stopped."

Despite the technological differences between our time and former times, humans have always had the same twenty-four hours in which to make choices about what matters in a given day; we have never been given all the time we'd like for deciding how to live our life.

In my thirties life seemed so perfect that I wished I could have hit the pause button and frozen it right there. The happiness I enjoyed with my first child was so perfect that I could have remained at that point in time forever. But, of course, she moved on and, with an education and good job with a big company, moved out. And now she's a grandmother!

Where did the years go? I find myself singing with Tevye, "Sunrise, sunset, Sunrise, sunset, Swiftly fly the years, One season following another, Laden with happiness and tears."

Life moves so swiftly that every day demands decisions that must be made on that day. Perhaps we can make some of those decisions tomorrow, but they won't be quite the same decisions as they were today. And if we keep postponing certain decisions, we will lose the opportunity of making them altogether. Well wrote William Blake that "he who kisses joy as it flies by will live in eternity's sunrise."

So I can reflect upon this hymn at bedtime, and as I pause to ponder the swiftly moving stream of life, I ask myself such questions as:

What did I do today that will matter in the last moments of my life?

What decisions did I make that were good, or else, bad?

What have I learned today that can make tomorrow a better day?

In the "change and decay in all around I see," this hymn can help me to value those few simple things that have eternal meaning.

Most of all, especially at the end of a day when things have not gone well, it's helpful to remember those sad, bereaved disciples who walked along the road to Emmaus on the evening of the first Easter, grieving that all was lost.

They were the ones who first offered the prayer, "*Abide with us*: for it is toward evening, and the day is far spent" (Luke 24:29). Their prayer was answered as the risen Jesus entered their home and broke bread with them.

That same Jesus still answers that prayer and makes his home with us. No matter what a day may bring of joy or sorrow, health or illness, achievement or failure, we will never be alone at eventide.

Crown Him With Many Crowns

1 Crown him with ma - ny crowns, the Lamb up - on his throne.
2 Crown him the Lord of life, who tri - umphed o'er the grave,
3 Crown him the Lord of love; be - hold his hands and side,
4 Crown him the Lord of years, the po - ten - tate of time,

Hark! how the heaven - ly an - them drowns all mu - sic but its own.
and rose vic - to - rious in the strife for those he came to save;
rich wounds, yet vi - si - ble a - bove, in beau - ty glo - ri - fied;
cre - a - tor of the rol - ling spheres, in ef - fa - bly su - blime.

A - wake, my soul, and sing of him who died for thee,
his glo - ries now we sing who died and rose on high,
no an - gels in the sky can ful - ly bear that sight,
All hail, Re - dee - mer, hail! for thou hast died for me;

and hail him as thy match - less king through all e - ter - ni - ty.
who died e - ter - nal life to bring, and lives that death may die.
but down - ward bends their bur - ning eye at mys - te - ries so bright.
thy praise shall ne - ver, ne - ver fail through - out e - ter - ni - ty.

26

Crown Him With Many Crowns

It is quite a shift from the meditative and introspective "Abide With Me" to the joyous and regal hymn, "Crown Him With Many Crowns."

It was written by Matthew Bridges, based on the text from Revelation 19:12: "On his head were many crowns." The text refers to a heavenly horse's rider who is clearly a symbol of Christ.

Matthew Bridges was born in 1800 and died full of years at the age of ninety-four. He was raised in the Church of England. Early in his ministry he published a vitriolic attack on Roman Catholicism designed to show "the real origin of certain papal superstitions," but later he was influenced by John Henry Newman and the Oxford Movement. He eventually converted to Roman Catholicism.

He published a number of books on history, as well as poetry and hymns, including *Hymns of the Heart* and *The Passion of Jesus*. His ministry drew him to Canada, where he served for several years and died in Quebec in 1894.

The hymn was reworked by Godfrey Thring (1823–1903), a minister in the Church of England, who produced several volumes of hymns. Thring's revisions have meant that today's hymnals vary considerably in which stanzas, how many stanzas, and in what order the stanzas are sung.

The tune, "Diademata," is the Greek word for "crowns." It was composed by George J. Elvey, the same composer who wrote, "Come, Ye Thankful People, Come" (see pp. 172–73). One commentator has written about the tune that it "makes a magnificent setting for the text, march-like and joyful without ever becoming mechanical or strident."

This is another hymn that uses the imagery of kingship to describe Christ, and again it seems strange that we as Americans would make a hymn about royalty so popular and incorporate it so widely in our singing and piety. I think it suggests a basic human instinct for someone in our lives to be our ruler amidst all the conflicting allegiances of life, some transcendent presence that will be our guide and strength when we are confused and weak.

Anyone seized by Christ's disruption of human history and his triumph over it can sing with enthusiasm:

> Crown Him the Lord of years,
> The Potentate of time;
> Creator of the rolling spheres,
> Ineffably sublime.
> All hail, Redeemer, hail!
> For Thou hast died for me;
> Thy praise shall never, never fail
> Throughout eternity.

Meditation

The King Is Dead. Long Live the King!

My colleague observes that it is rather curious that so many hymns that speak of God as King remained popular in a young nation that had rid itself of British royalty in favor of government of the people, by the people, and for the people. But now we wonder if such hymns will survive by the end of the present century in a culture in which all of this "king stuff" is questioned by those who, rightly, call for language that is gender-inclusive.

Will there arise a new generation of hymn writers who find new ways to express what the old hymns were attempting to say? I hope so, but I raise a different question: if we succeed in finding new words for the old hymns, will the old way of faith and life under the heavenly King continue to be practiced in some relevant manner?

So let me engage in some old-fashioned memories.

With the exception of my Uncle Will (about whom I have written in another of these meditations), during the 1930s when I was a little kid, my parents, uncles, and aunts no longer worshiped at the church in which I had been baptized. They had all moved to another town twenty miles away; however, their non-attendance was *not* dictated by the distance from the old church.

The old church had been built by the owner of the iron mill for his workers. A special transept of the sanctuary was reserved for the mill owner and his family so that, during worship, he could gaze benevolently upon his workers, as though those immigrants were his subjects.

However, when the owner died and steel replaced iron so that the mill was closed, the special transept was vacant during worship and there was no longer any need to be present so as to be patronized by the mill owner and his family. Understandably, worship attendance, like the mill, went into decline.

Still, on every Sunday, we traveled back to my grandmother's house atop the hill above the church for Sunday dinner, and here's the interesting point. We were all dressed for church! The men wore their "Sunday best" with white starched collars and neckties, with the women similarly attired as though for worship. The old snapshots reveal that even I wore a necktie.

So what was going on? Even if we could not have "put it into words" we believed that our lives were being lived under a higher, sovereign Majesty, and that made a profound difference.

There was Someone worthy of our getting "dressed up" for. Even though we were of the laboring class, life under a higher Majesty demanded that we recognize special occasions of dignity with appropriately respectable dress. Just take a look at the old photos of immigrant wedding couples!

Even outside the walls of the church, we knew that God's majesty was always calling us to a life attitude of reverence, reverence above all for God, but also for marriage and the family.

It would never have occurred to us, as is often the practice nowadays, to dress up for a business meeting at which a large sale was pending, but then dress down in our shorts and sandals for church. We did not feel casual in the presence of almighty God.

There was one day of the week that had been given to all humanity for Sabbath rest. It was given not only to Christians, but to all persons, even to our sisters and brothers of the animal realm, to our beasts of burden.

We hadn't heard of Albert Schweitzer but already knew something of his central principal of "reverence for life." Thus, we knew that our Higher Majesty was a friendly, caring God. But while we knew that God was our friend, we would never have thought of God as our pal.

We realized also that there was a special majesty attached to our need for play, but not in the sense of the outrageous expenditure of huge amounts of money upon professional athletic events or of over-organized Sunday sports schedules for children.

On Sundays, we had time for quiet play with one another, for walks in the countryside, for fishing at the mill pond at the bottom of the hill, or for table games like dominoes at sunset. We didn't go to the movies on Sunday; we knew we needed one day away from the silver screen, just as many of us now could benefit from one day away from Facebook.

Of course, the good ole' days were not totally good. There were silly blue laws and petty legalisms. But as I remember those Sundays, even after having experienced many great Sundays in my more than half century in the pulpit, it is interesting that my best memories of Sunday are not in church, but at my grandmother's home. It was entirely natural therefore that, when darkness had fallen and we sat on the front porch, we sang together the old hymns, so many of which adored God as our King.

So find new language and write new hymns to express this reverence and adoration with new words. I'll sing along with you. But don't ever lose that way of life that is lived under a higher Majesty. Long live the King!

There's a Wideness in God's Mercy

1 There's a___ wide-ness in God's mer - cy like the wide - ness of the sea;
2 There is___ wel-come for the___ sin - ner and more gra - ces for the good;
3 For the___ love of God is___ broa - der than the mea - sure of our mind;
4 If our___ love were but more___ sim - ple, we would take him at his word,

there's a___ kind - ness in his jus - tice which is more than___ li - ber - ty.
there is___ mer - cy___ with the___ Sav - ior; there is heal - ing___ in his blood.
and the___ heart of___ the E - ter - nal is most won - der - ful - ly kind.
and our___ lives would be il - lu-mined by the pre - sence of our Lord.

27

There's a Wideness in God's Mercy

This is a beautiful theological hymn, set to a rollicking Dutch melody.

It was written by Frederick William Faber. Like other hymn writers in this book, he was an Anglican priest who was heavily influenced by John Henry Newman and the Oxford Movement, which sought to reclaim the richness of the Catholic tradition. Like Matthew Bridges (pp. 187), he converted to Roman Catholicism. He was born in 1814 to Calvinist parents in Yorkshire. He was educated at Oxford University and ordained as an Anglican priest in 1839 and as a Roman Catholic priest only seven years later.

He wrote 150 hymns, all after he converted to Catholicism. Having grown up in evangelical Protestantism, he sought to bring to Roman Catholic worship the joy of congregational singing. Some of his hymns, one scholar has written, "are unsurpassed as specimens of the highest order of devotional poetry—lofty in thought, elegant in diction, graceful in rhythm, fervent in spirit, highly suggestive, and wonderfully inspiring."

Faber wrote this hymn in the midst of his missionary work during the nineteenth-century famines in Ireland and England; he named it "Come to Jesus."

The tune, "In Babilone," comes from a Dutch songbook of the early eighteenth century. The harmony comes from a Dutchman, Julius Röntgen, and it appeared first in *The English Hymnal* in 1906 and then in Röntgen's collection called *Old Dutch Peasant Songs and Country Dances Transcribed for the Piano* in 1912.

Röntgen was born in Leipzig in 1855 and studied music there, but he spent most of his career in Holland. He served as professor at the Amsterdam Conservatory and then conductor of the Society for the Advancement of Musical Art. Later he returned to the Amsterdam Conservatory, where he served as its director, and in his retirement he devoted himself to composing music. He died at Utrecht in 1932.

At first glance, this might seem a strange hymn to be included in some hymnals. For example, the Calvinist heritage, with its historic emphasis on predestination, would probably be uncomfortable with a hymn that celebrates "a wideness in God's mercy." Even in other traditions that reject predestination, there is debate about who really qualifies for God's everlasting mercy.

Faber rejected the idea that some people qualify for God's love and others don't. One of Faber's stanzas that didn't make it into some contemporary hymnals goes as follows:

But we make His love too narrow
By false limits of our own;
And we magnify His strictness
With a zeal He will not own.

Several years ago, the American Bible Society published a controversial version of the New Testament that substituted the word "kindness" for "grace." The Society argued that the term "grace" had lost its meaning for contemporary people, and "kindness" was the best replacement. Actually, that *is* closer to the Hebrew word for God's grace—which is "loving kindness."

So, here it is. The setting is hunger and famine. The theme is the inclusive love of a God who is overwhelmingly kind. After centuries of hostilities between Protestants and Catholics, this is a hymn written by a Roman Catholic to a tune by a Dutch Protestant and used today by both traditions.

For those who are burdened by guilt, for those plagued by thoughts of divine judgment, for those suffering in poverty and deprivation, this is a hymn which declares:

There's a wideness in God's mercy,
Like the wideness of the sea;
There's a kindness in God's justice,
Which is more than liberty.

Meditation

Someone's Praying, Lord

Whenever I sing this hymn, I find myself asking, "Yes, but just how wide?"

Christians of all stripes have never agreed about the exact breadth of acceptance that God's wayward and wandering children will finally face. Sincere followers of Jesus, persons of good faith, disagree about the dimensions of divine love.

Some believe that "the tree lies where it falls," that our present life constitutes the day of salvation and that, having had our opportunity to repent and believe during our earthly life, there remains hereafter, a final and irreversible judgment.

Others believe that the door of decision could never be closed upon any of God's wayward children and cite those hopeful words of the closing chapters of our New Testament that promise us that the gates of the New Jerusalem shall never be shut.

I won't try to resolve these differences, but my experience is that one can find believers in both camps whose lives demonstrate such a depth of kindness and unconditional love as to convince me that there must be, indeed, a wideness in God's mercy.

I have not found a more assuring answer to our questions than the hymn of this faithful priest who urges us to sing,

> For the love of God is broader
> Than the measures of the mind;
> And the heart of the Eternal
> Is most wonderfully kind.

Perhaps the best theology is that which begins by reminding us that we can never outdo the God whose love, mercy, kindness, and justice will exceed our wildest imagination.

But how then shall we live with such an expansive view of God's mercy?

George MacDonald (1824–1905), Victorian mythmaker, novelist, poet, and preacher, would often tell his own life story in his novels' characters. In his novel, *Weighed and Wanting*, he expresses his discomfort with the doctrines of limited atonement and unconditional election that were proclaimed from the Scottish pulpit of his day by saying, "I well remember . . . feeling as a child that I did not care for God to love me if he did not love everybody: the kind of love I needed was the love that all men needed, the love that belonged to their nature as the children of the Father, a love he could not give me except he gave it to all men."

We can all relate to such feelings. A God who has special favorites might turn out to be a God out of whose special favor I myself might fall some day. We all yearn for a God who hears the deepest prayers and longings of every one of us, however imperfect we may be. Whatever we may believe about the afterlife, we all want desperately to believe that now, in our life on earth today,

> There is no place where earth's sorrows
> Are more felt that up in heaven;
> There is no place where earth's failings
> Have such kindly judgment given.

Let me tell you what I often ponder during the still watches of the night.

We live within sight and sound of the intersection of two busy interstate highways. As I am often granted at my age what a dear Scottish lady called "God's gift of sleepless nights that I might be all the more in prayer," I wonder what people are praying as they speed along those highways, carrying on the restless commerce of humankind.

Some trucker is praying for his wife and little boy. Twelve more hours on the road until he'll deliver his load and be with them again. Why has he ended up in a job that takes him away from his family? "Lord, be with my Martha and little Tommy, and help me to make it through this long night!"

A middle-aged biker roars through the night on his Harley. He has had too much to drink, and he knows it, even though he has promised himself before to cut back on the booze. "Jesus, I can't see straight! Please, just get me home safely tonight, and I promise I'll never do this again."

An ambulance screams as it heads to the hospital in Sarasota. Loved ones pray for their aged mother who has had another stroke, "Dear Lord, give her comfort and relieve her fears. If this is the end, let it be peaceful for her."

And then I hear the whistle and clatter of the railroad train that makes its way toward the nearby port to deliver its goods to the freighter that will head out to sea at dawn. "One more month and I'll be retiring," thinks the engineer, "but then what? What's the purpose of my life anyway? Lord, is there a central station toward which my long journey is headed?"

I was once taught to pray for every person whom I met throughout the day. I still try to observe that practice; however, I'm working at a new one. Whenever I meet anyone, even if it's the brief encounter with the checkout lady at the supermarket, I wonder what they're praying about, because I've come to believe that more people are praying than we could ever realize.

Paul Claudel (1868–1955) wrote these unforgettable words about the universality of prayer:"There is no one of my brothers . . . I can do without. . . . In the heart of the meanest miser, the most squalid prostitute, the most miserable drunkard, there is an immortal soul with holy aspirations, which deprived of daylight, worships in the night. I hear them speaking when I speak and weeping when I go down on my knees. There is no one of them I can do without. . . . I need them all in my praise of God. There are many living souls but there is not one of them with whom I am not in communion in the sacred apex where we utter together the Our Father."

We are never alone when we pray; we are part of the great family of the One whom Jesus taught us to call "Our Father." Just this realization can save me from thinking of myself and my final destiny as one of God's favorites.

So as you begin or end your day, try remembering the words of the African American spiritual, "Someone's praying, Lord." We find ourselves thinking new, hopeful thoughts about others when we remember that they, too, are children of God's worldwide family of prayer.

The Church's One Foundation

1 The Church's one foun - da - tion is Je - sus Christ her Lord;
2 E - lect from ev - ery na - tion, yet one o'er all the earth,
3 Though with a scorn - ful won - der we see her sore op - pressed,
4 'Mid toil and tri - bu - la - tion, and tu - mult of her war,
5 Yet she on earth hath u - nion with God, the Three in One,

she is his new cre - a - tion, by wa - ter and the word:
her char - ter of sal - va - tion: one Lord, one faith, one birth;
by schisms rent a - sun - der, by he - re - sies dis - tressed:
she waits the con - sum - ma - tion of peace for - e - ver - more,
and my - stic sweet com - mu - nion With those whose rest is won:

from heaven he came and sought her to be his ho - ly bride;
one ho - ly name she bles - ses, par - takes one ho - ly food,
yet saints their watch are keep - ing, their cry goes up, "How long?"
till with the vi - sion glo - rious her long - ing eyes are blest,
O hap - py ones and ho - ly! Lord, give us grace that we,

with his own blood he bought her, and for her life he died.
and to one hope she pres - ses with ev - ery grace en - dued.
and soon the night of weep - ing shall be the morn of song.
and the great Church vic - to - rious shall be the Church at rest.
like them, the meek and low - ly, on high may dwell with thee.

28

The Church's One Foundation

This hymn is one of the most beloved hymns in Protestant Christianity.

It was written by Samuel John Stone, who was born in Whitmore, Staffordshire, England in 1839 and died in 1900. He was educated in London and at Oxford University and was ordained as an Anglican priest. Throughout his long parish ministry, he wrote several books and served on the committee that produced *Hymns Ancient and Modern*.

His father was also an Anglican priest, and eventually he succeeded his father as vicar of St. Paul's in Haggerston, London.

Stone was known as "the poor man's pastor." For the last ten years of his life he served All-Hallows-on-the-Wall in London, which he turned into a refuge for working girls and women. He was known to protect the women with his own hands and at risk to his own safety. He combined "virility and sympathy," and his doctor said about him, "He had the muscles of a prize fighter and the nerves of a violin."

His ministry in London was summed up as follows: "He created a beautiful place of worship for the humble folk and made it a center of light in dark places."

The tune "Aurelia," suggesting "golden," was composed by one of the greatest church musicians in English history, Samuel Sebastian Wesley, who was born in 1810 and died in 1876. Music was in his genes, for his grandfather was the incomparable hymn writer and cofounder of Methodism, Charles Wesley.

Samuel Sebastian Wesley is considered one of the greatest composers in the English cathedral tradition, which includes Henry Purcell. At the age of ten, he was the chorister at the

Chapel Royal and by sixteen he was a church organist. He received a Doctor of Music degree from Oxford University when he was only twenty-nine.

Wesley was an avid fisherman, and it is said that he accepted music appointments on the basis of the availability of good waters in which to fish. Reportedly he once had an assistant play a dedicatory concert because he was fishing, and he told the assistant to advise everyone that he was unavoidably detained.

"The Church's One Foundation" arose out of Stone's defense of orthodoxy and a pastoral concern that his congregation learn the basics of Christian doctrine; in this case, it was the article in the Apostle's Creed, which reads: "I believe in the Holy Catholic Church, the communion of saints."

The prominent hymnologist John Julian declared the hymn "magnificent." However, because of its widespread use on official church occasions, Archbishop William Temple became exceedingly tired of it and complained that it followed him everywhere he went.

Like much of the church today, the historical setting for this hymn was one of controversy. The battle was known as the Colenso Affair in the Church of England, and it reached its peak in 1866. The Anglican Bishop of Natal in South Africa was John Colenso, who made critical statements about the historicity of some parts of the Bible and raised questions about various Christian doctrines.

Colenso was a courageous missionary in South Africa and did much to improve the lives of the South African population. He refused to accept the idea that the ancestors of newly Christianized South Africans were doomed to eternal damnation. But his opposition to British imperialism ultimately brought him more colonial enemies than his opponents within the church.

In the midst of this turmoil, the Reverend Samuel John Stone back in England vehemently defended the orthodoxy of

the church and wrote this famous hymn. The third stanza refers
to the controversy:

> Though with a scornful wonder
> This world sees her oppressed,
> By schisms rent asunder,
> By heresies distressed,
> Yet saints their watch are keeping;
> Their cry goes up: "How long?"
> And soon the night of weeping
> Shall be the morn of song.

Even though he was critical of Colenso, Stone saw the
negative effects of the church's preoccupation with controversy,
and he longed for that day when the church would be unified
again. This is how the hymn ends:

> Yet she on earth hath union
> With God the Three in One,
> And mystic sweet communion
> With those who rest is won:
> O happy ones and holy!
> Lord, give us grace that we,
> Like them, the meek and lowly,
> May live eternally.

May all of us say that prayer for the church in our day and
all the days to come.

Meditation

Mystic Sweet Communion

Many longstanding church members look up from their hymnals as they sing this ever-popular hymn; entire verses are em-
bedded in their memory. Still, I've often wanted to ask them

how they understand the words, "Yet mystic sweet communion with those whose rest is won."

If I could interview them as they file out of church on a Sunday morning, I'd also ask what they're thinking when they recite the words of the Apostles' Creed in which they affirm their belief in "the communion of saints."

The assumption of this hymn and of that statement in the creed is that the church on earth is somehow in touch with the church in heaven, with "those whose rest is won." My guess is that the responses to my question would be "all over the map."

Those with a Roman Catholic background might find it natural to assume that we have some continuing connection with the great saints and spiritual heroes of the past; in their upbringing they would have remembered special days for remembrance of certain saints—especially St. Patrick's Day, if they were Irish.

And the Protestants? Even if they wear green on that day, their standard answer to my question would be that "we don't actually do that"; we don't observe saints' days. Still, we go on singing this hymn and reciting the creed in which we affirm some tie with "those to glory gone," as in the words of one of Charles Wesley's hymns.

It's just as difficult to pin down theologians in their answer to my question.

Biblical scholars would say that there's not much light to be found in the New Testament on the question of how faithful Christians who have died are joined in communion with Christians on earth. Inferences of the connection can be made from two or three verses, but no fully developed doctrine is provided.

Still, evidence of some continuing ties, especially with martyrs, begins to appear on tombs and in the catacombs by the late third century and, as the centuries proceed, prayer to the saints begins to be the standard practice of popular devotion.

Leaving aside the unresolved discussion of the scholars, it seems as though we just can't get it "out of our system" that we have some relationship with our loved ones who have passed on to the other side.

At least, I can't.

Even if I can't justify my practice biblically or theologically, I have a list of those who are "my saints" at the end of the little prayer list that I carry in my pocket. Let me be clear; I don't pray to them. The names of these twenty-one dear souls are written there to keep them in daily memory.

They're an interesting bunch, and have little in common with one another. One of them never finished school while others earned advanced degrees. Nearly all of them were regular in church attendance, but one of them hardly ever darkened the door of a church as an adult. One attained world fame, but most were unknown outside their own hometown. A few were wealthy, but one was almost penniless. They certainly didn't vote the same political party line, and probably would have given different answers to my question about the communion of saints.

But they had one common characteristic: each one of them reflected some facet of God's glory. In some one way, each of them taught me something about what it might mean to live my life as a follower of Jesus and a child of my heavenly Father.

And so, what do I do with my list? Because each one of them helps me concentrate upon some specific skill that I need to improve, I take one of them with me as my companion for a given day.

Jim W. and Edwin D. remind me to be a good listener. The memory of Ken teaches me to endure suffering patiently. Charlotte's life tells me to let "the law of kindness" be always upon my lips. Anne and Jane rebuke me when I lapse into some intemperate way. Norton shows me how to be a healing presence. Fred and Will remind me to live simply, and Freddy always rumbles with laughter at my self-seriousness.

I can hear someone saying, "Why don't you just take Jesus with you every day instead of one of those frail and fallible human saints?"

My answer is simple: I've learned that I can make Jesus into whatever I want him to be. But I can't do that with my saints; I can never forget exactly where and how their lives would correct, support, encourage, or even be critical of mine. And so, I take them with me for an entire day and, at the end of the day, give thanks that, indeed, "the memory of the righteous is a blessing."

If you'll try making your own list of saints, you'll find that you can always have "mystic sweet communion" with them, especially on discouraging days. As a young preacher, on many a snowy Sunday morning when attendance was low and my discouragement high, I would remember that there was always a larger multitude somehow present in that barren sanctuary.

What power I found in those final words of the communion prayer, "Therefore with angels and archangels and *all the company of heaven*, we worship and adore Thy glorious name, evermore praising Thee and saying: Holy, Holy, Holy, Lord God of Hosts; Heaven and earth are full of Thy glory; Glory be to Thee, O Lord Most High."